# The Ethics
of
Public Service

**Recent Titles in**
**Contributions in Political Science**
*Series Editor: Bernard K. Johnpoll*

# THE ETHICS
# OF
# PUBLIC SERVICE

## RESOLVING MORAL DILEMMAS
## IN PUBLIC ORGANIZATIONS

Kathryn G. Denhardt

CONTRIBUTIONS IN POLITICAL SCIENCE, NUMBER 195

GREENWOOD PRESS
NEW YORK · WESTPORT, CONNECTICUT · LONDON

**Library of Congress Cataloging-in-Publication Data**

Denhardt, Kathryn G.
   The ethics of public service.

   (Contributions in political science, ISSN 0147-1066 ;
no. 195)
   Bibliography: p.
   Includes index.
   1. Public administration—Moral and ethical aspects.
I. Title.  II. Series.
JF1525.E8D46     1988     172'.2     87-15060
ISBN 0-313-25517-2 (lib. bdg. : alk. paper)

British Library Cataloguing in Publication Data is available.

Library of Congress Catalog Card Number: 87-15060
ISBN: 0-313-25517-2
ISSN: 0147-1066

First published in 1988

Greenwood Press, Inc.
88 Post Road West, Westport, Connecticut 06881

Printed in the United States of America

# CONTENTS

# PREFACE

There is no clear consensus about what constitutes ethical administrative behavior and what that means for public administration. Should concern lie primarily with corruption, with the administrative role in the policy-making process, with the conflicting obligations of administrators, or with other dimensions of administrative activity?. These concerns and many others find their place in the eclectic administrative ethics literature. What is lacking is a theoretical framework which would link, coordinate, and guide administrative ethics research and practice. Without such a theoretical framework, the field will remain disjointed, often incomprehensible, and will fail to develop and progress adequately. Thus, the first objective of this book is to help lay the groundwork for a theoretical framework from which the theory and practice of ethics in public administration can be guided.

In addition to the absence of an agreed-upon theoretical framework for administrative ethics, the field has failed to take advantage of the philosophical traditions that should be underpinnings of any study or application of ethics. These philosophical traditions include both *ethics as a branch of philosophy* (which deals with how to identify, deliberate, and resolve ethical problems), and *political philosophy* (which has much to say to current public administration about the appropriate roles, behaviors, and values of administrators). Not only would the further development of the philosophical traditions be *helpful* to the field, but it is also *necessary* in that by focusing only on the current state of public administration the field risks developing a narrowly interpreted, self-serving ethic which will neither survive the test of time nor serve the public interest. Therefore, a second objective for this book is to delineate the place of philosophy in administrative ethics, though it will be left to other works yet to come to fully develop this dimension.

Finally, there has been too little emphasis placed on understanding the important dimensions of practicing administrative ethics *in an organizational setting*. The modern organization as a context for ethical behavior provides a new set of obligations, constraints, and pressures which cannot be adequately considered if only the ethics of individuals are addressed. To deal with the ethical behavior of individual administrators without dealing with the context of their organizational role provides ethical guidance that will be irrelevant in practice in many situations. Thus, the third objective of this book is to establish the importance of developing ethical public *organizations* along with ethical public administrators.

These three objectives provide the basis on which this work is organized. In Chapter 1 a conceptual framework is developed, drawing on the existing literature in the field, and establishing what is, in effect, the operational conception of administrative ethics. This framework will not reflect any one of the major pieces of research, but will instead be a compilation of what seems to be shared and what each uniquely adds to the understanding of how public administration ethics should be studied and practiced. Then this framework will be examined in terms of its soundness from the broader perspectives of our philosophical traditions, and in terms of how it fits with the role and context of public administration in the general society (Chapter 2) and in public organizations (Chapter 3).

Chapters 4 and 5 address the shortcomings of the current state of public administration ethics, and propose ways in which development of the field can be enhanced from the point of view of the individual administrator and then from the point of view of the public organization. Chapter 6 tests the reasonableness of the theoretical framework and the suggestions of earlier chapters by applying them to a specific case that might be faced by an administrator. This provides not only an opportunity to critique the emerging theoretical framework, but also an illustration of how ethical dilemmas can be identified, deliberated over, and a decision made—thus serving as a pedagogical tool.

What this book does *not* deal with directly is issues of corruption. Though corruption is a very important problem for public administration (Truelson, 1986; Rose-Ackerman, 1978), there seems to be little disagreement that corrupt acts are unethical. The problems of corruption in public administration are not problems of defining what is ethical—the fact that corruption is unethical is agreed upon. Thus, issues of corruption do little to inform the development of a theoretical framework encompassing the broad ranges of ethical behavior expected of public administrators. However, the framework for analysis and deliberation that is developed here can be applied to questions of corruption, just as it can be applied to the day-to-day decisions of administrators, which is the focus of this book.

What is sought through the writing of this book is the development of an approach to the study and practice of administrative ethics that is based on a better-developed theoretical framework, is more grounded in philosophy, and is ultimately more practical in that it considers and accommodates the exigencies of the environment in which public administrators must practice—the modern public organization.

I am deeply indebted to John Rohr, Terry Cooper, James Bowman, and Ralph Chandler for their leadership in the development of this field of inquiry, and for the open exchange of views I have been fortunate to engage in with them. I have benefited greatly from the comments and substantive contributions of John Nalbandian, James Bowman, Elaine Sharp, and Marvin Harder at various stages in the development of this book. Finally, I want to thank my husband, Robert Denhardt, for his ongoing intellectual stimulation and extraordinary levels of personal support, both of which were essential to the completion of this book. While I accept personal responsibility for what has been written, I gratefully accept and acknowledge the help of others along the way.

# 1

# PUBLIC ADMINISTRATION ETHICS: DEVELOPING A FRAMEWORK

Ethics in public administration suffers from the absence of a theoretical framework to supply focus, definition, background, and a common frame of reference for the research and practice of ethical administration. No paradigm presently exists to provide a shared understanding of what "ethics" means when applied to the field of public administration.

There seems to be little disagreement that such a framework is lacking. Examining three works that reflect on the "state of the discipline," we see little change in recent years. In 1980, Dwight Waldo described the state of moral and ethical behavior in public administration as *"chaotic"* (Waldo, 1980:100). In 1983, James Bowman stated that "in both practice and theory, the ethical implications of administrative and political conduct remain largely unexplored" (Bowman, 1983a:71). And most recently, John Rohr, in presenting a "state of the discipline" report at a major conference, states that "throughout this report I have stressed the diversity in the ethics field; a diversity that comes close to chaos" (Rohr, 1986a:53). Though he goes on to identify some areas of emerging consensus, it is notable that in six years administrative ethics progressed only from a state of chaos to something "close to chaos" in the eyes of those most involved in the field. That failure to develop is directly related to the lack of an agreed-upon theoretical framework by which administrative ethics research and practice might be guided.

Since public administration has been practiced for many centuries, and has been an acknowledged discipline since Wilson's "The Study of Administration" (Wilson, 1887) a century ago, the absence of a theoretical framework for public administration ethics requires some explanation. It is not the case that public administrators have acted without a sense of ethics during those centuries. Nor is it necessarily true that events in recent years show that the ethics of public servants has deteriorated. Rather, the nature of public administration, the role of public administrators, and societal expectations have gradually evolved to a point that makes it necessary for us to return our attention to administrative ethics and to the changes these new developments could require.

The nature of public administration has changed as public policies and government activity have grown in complexity, accompanied by greater discretionary authority being placed with public administrators. But, those same factors were of concern to Woodrow Wilson a century ago when he called for reforms in public administration. Wilson's solutions to these problems (a politics/administration dichotomy and greater professional independence for public administrators) are now deemed inadequate as a theoretical base for administrative ethics practice and research, and actually helped create the conditions in modern organizations that foster some of the major ethical concerns in public administration today.

What has changed since Wilson's time are the arrangements of complex modern organizations that now accompany the increasing complexity of government policy and the prevalence of administrative discretion. This makes it incumbent upon us to advance the ethical nature of administrators and public organizations or resign ourselves to an administrative state that is truly out of control and unhindered by the ethical precepts of society. In addition, there is an increased sense of professionalism among public administrators which is accompanied by a demand for guidance from that profession about the ethical role of the administrator—guidance that has not been sufficiently provided by civil service reforms, nor the various codes of ethics and conflict of interest laws which have resulted from the latest surge in interest in public sector ethics.

Not only does a theoretical framework for administrative ethics need to be developed, but there is also a need to outline the *practical* purposes to which the framework and resulting research can be put. Four such purposes can be identified: to emphasize the need for ethical deliberation in *all* administrative decisions; to provide procedural and normative guidance for administrators in making those decisions; to foster organizational environments which permit and encourage ethical behavior; and finally, to aid in the process of holding administrators and public organizations accountable.

The purposes outlined above differ from most approaches to administrative ethics in that equal attention will be paid to the *individual administrator* and the *public organization*. A number of people have argued that modern bureaucracies encourage amorality on the part of organization members (e.g., Hummel, 1977), but for them the solution is usually seen as changing the nature of the organization, which is then thought to result in ethical and moral behavior. Others, whose focus has been on the behavior of the individual administrator, approach administrative ethics with the individual as the sole area of concern. In this book it will be argued that focusing on individual ethical development *or* on organizational reform will inevitably fail to achieve the desired result of a more ethical public administration. Instead, the organizational context and the individual development of the administrator must *both* be integral parts of any approach to administrative ethics.

Developing the framework for administrative ethics involves a delineation of the extant paradigm. According to Thomas Kuhn (1970), the function of a paradigm is to provide a field with concrete models, resulting in overt agreement on fundamentals and a commitment to the same rules and standards. Clearly, research and practice of administrative ethics would benefit from some effort to discern such a foundation. The general approach will be, first, to establish as nearly as possible the models, fundamentals, rules and standards which have guided recent research in administrative ethics. Then, this extant paradigm, or operational framework, will be subjected to critique from a variety of perspectives in order to refine it. In the next section, an overview and analysis of recent work in administrative ethics will be presented.

## ETHICS IN PUBLIC ADMINISTRATION LITERATURE

While Plato's *Republic* might be argued to be the best starting point in studying administrative ethics, we will instead begin with a look at more recent works in order to establish the current state of administrative ethics, and to build a framework from that point. This framework will be developed by interpreting early writings and then following the changes through the more recent works, in the process creating a series of statements that will culminate in what might be considered the operational (though unstated) framework currently guiding the field.

This statement of the operational framework is not an end in itself. It is a bringing together of various ideas in a complex field which will then be analyzed and critiqued from different perspectives. The result of this exploration will be suggestions for achieving a more ethical, and perhaps more accountable, public administration, as well as illuminating areas in need of further research attention.

### The 1940's

This discussion will begin with Wayne A. R. Leys (1944) because his work represents one of the earliest explicit treatments of ethics as it relates to modern bureaucracy in the United States, and it appeared about the same time that the Wilsonian politics/administration dichotomy was being challenged (this challenge is very important to any understanding of the practice of public administration ethics, and will be discussed in more detail in chapter 2).

Leys discussed ethics in terms of making good public policy decisions. He argues that *custom* is often used as a substitute for thinking through the problems of public policy that confront us. He suggested that we often find it "much easier to say that each generation is endowed with the wisdom of the past than . . . to find the traditional precepts that solve some of our problems" (Leys, 1944:9). When faced with new areas in which to make public policy decisions (unemployment insurance, fair telephone rates, and minimum airplane altitudes are a few mentioned by Leys as being important in the 1940's), custom can often be inappropriate or misleading, and policymakers must seek new alternatives.

Though Leys pointed out the deficiencies of relying exclusively on custom in making all policy decisions, he also recognized that individuals often experience "a feeling of presumptiveness and hesitancy whenever you undertake to evaluate things in the name of your own judgment rather than in the name of hoary customs and sacred traditions" (Leys, 1944:12). He sought to relieve us of those feelings of presumptiveness by pointing out that our ancestors did not leave us with customs that could provide all the necessary guidance in addressing modern problems, but they did leave us with "arts and sciences which tell us *how* we may go about the business of thinking for ourselves" (Leys, 1944:12). He lists *ethics* as one of the fields that serve as "sources of doubt" regarding custom and tradition. Ethics raises critical questions about existing policies, and this process of questioning may help counteract the inertia of time-honored customs and unsatisfactory policies.

In a later book that dealt with the more specific topic of making policy *decisions*, Leys explicitly defined ethics as "the study of standards for decision making" (Leys, 1952:4) and discusses how ethics can be applied to making decisions about policy issues. "Ethics, as a discipline of questions, should unparalyze the mind at the moment of action. It suggests the unremembered or unperceived angles that may need investigation. . . . It does not supply factual information, but is a reminder of the kinds of facts that may need investigating" (Leys, 1952:11). He explores the many systems of ethics developed over the centuries, summarizes the critical questions that each system has raised, and discusses how each might serve as a guide to policymakers who must question existing policy or create new policies (Leys, 1952:189-191).

This view of how ethics can serve public administration provides a model or framework for ethical action in public administration as it was understood in the 1940's:

*Model I—The 1940's*

To be ethical requires that an administrator examine and question the standards by which administrative decisions are made rather than relying exclusively on custom and tradition.

Leys' focus is on the policy decision maker, and the implicit assumption seems to be that the policymaker is an elected official, or at least quite high in the bureaucratic hierarchy. Perhaps that explains why his work has not figured as prominently in recent administrative ethics research as it might have. However, in light of current views regarding the significant role played by administrators in the policy-making process (e.g., Lipsky, 1980; Davis, 1969), Leys' work is very relevant for the present-day administrator.

Another distinguishing characteristic of Leys' view of ethical behavior is its philosophical leanings, an orientation which some in the field have considered to be impractical for public administration. Perhaps because of this need to emphasize relevance and practicality, public administration has generally avoided philosophy (moral or political) in discussions of administrative ethics, but Leys' work is a good example of how philosophy can be an important and necessary addition to both ethics scholarship and ethical practice.

**The 1950's**

In 1953, Hurst R. Anderson, then president of The American University, delivered a speech to the Society for Personnel Administration on the topic of "Ethical Values in Administration." In his speech, Dr. Anderson discussed a point which is crucial to the field of administrative ethics:

I don't see how it is possible for the individual who is an administrator in this period to divorce the technique of administration from a fundamental philosophy of personal and social life. You can do it in a superficial sense, but every time you make a decision about an administrative problem, or any time you seek to resolve an administrative tension, you have to resolve it in terms of some assumptions that lie at the heart of what we may call a philosophy of personal and social living. (Anderson, 1954:2)

His purpose in giving the speech was "to point out the fundamental relationship between the ethical principles or assumptions upon which we all live and work and the problem of administration" (Anderson, 1954:1). In the process of accomplishing this task, Anderson takes an approach that differs from Leys in two basic ways. First, Anderson asserts that ethical questions are important in *all* administrative decisions, not just those intended to formulate public policy. Second, Anderson conceives of ethics as the assumptions that guide the lives and work of all of us.

These differences are important because Anderson's work implies a much broader scope of what is "ethically relevant." He states that all administrative decisions are based on some implicit, often unexamined assumptions (or decision standards). If we can identify and study these assumptions, then perhaps we can "agree upon . . . the foundation upon which to construct a philosophy and technique of administration" which is ethical (Anderson, 1954:3). Anderson suggests that the basic assumptions administrators hold are probably widely shared and he goes on to discuss ten core values upon which we operate as a society, including: the significance in the individual human personality; common consent as a basis for social action; and devotion to truth (Anderson, 1954:4). The ten core values will not be discussed in detail here, but the fact that he could list such values has significance for the development of administrative ethics. In addition to providing a "source of doubt," an approach to administrative ethics that specifies core values might provide more adequate guidance for administrative decisions.

In light of Anderson's work the framework for understanding ethical action can be refined as follows:

### Model II—The 1950's

To be ethical requires that an administrator examine and question the standards, or assumptions, by which administrative decisions are made. The standards should reflect to some degree the core values of our society though not relying exclusively on custom and tradition.

### The 1960's

The 1960's brought about a new focus in the study of administrative ethics. It was a time of rethinking the role of the individual and the role of institutions, and exploring the possibilities for change. In *Men, Management, and Morality* (1965) Robert T. Golembiewski sets out to discover and explicate "specific organizational arrangements and techniques that violate the traditional theory of organization and also respect the Judeo-Christian Ethic, while they contribute to high levels of output and high employee satisfaction" (Golembiewski, 1965:60). He describes principles associated with the traditional theory of organization as "one way" authority, detailed supervision, respect only for the physiological properties of individuals, and routinized work at the lowest levels (Golembiewski, 1965:66). Considering the traditional theory of organization unnecessarily limiting to individual freedom, he sought a new organization ethic to replace the traditional one. This marks an important turning point in administrative ethics in that the influence of the organization is explicitly acknowledged.

In the course of his work, Golembiewski makes another important contribution when he points out distinctions among the concepts of conduct, ethics, and morals.

"Conduct" refers simply to the observed behavior of individuals or groups of individuals. "Ethics," in turn refers to the contemporary standards at any point in time in terms of which men evaluate their conduct and that of men about them. "Morals," finally, refers to absolute standards that exist beyond time, standards of the good and the true. (Golembiewski, 1965:61)

The implication of this distinction is that "ethics," while being the contemporary standard of right conduct, may well change with time as a better understanding of absolute moral standards becomes evident. A second implication is that while *absolute* standards might not be known, *ethical* standards, at any given time, *can* be known. This seems consistent with Anderson's views about known standards, but differs from Leys who defined ethics as the study of standards for decision making, thus implying a constant process of discovery rather than a known quantity. In fact, questioning and being critical are integral parts of being "ethical" in Leys' terms, while Anderson's and Golembiewski's conceptions indicate that an administrator can be ethical if he or she is able to discern what the standards of acceptable conduct are, and then act accordingly.

A subtle, but key issue in the development of administrative ethics is this question of whether being ethical means discovering the content or substance of social values (i.e., being able to identify and then follow the standards) or, alternatively, whether questioning the existing ethical standards is a necessary part of ethical action. The answer hinges on whether we can actually identify the substantive content of our social values and call those our "ethical standards," and then, whether those social values should be open to a process of questioning, debate, and change. For now we will incorporate Golembiewski's view of changing ethical standards into our developing framework but continue to explore those issues in this chapter and in subsequent chapters.

## Model III—The 1960's

To be ethical requires that an administrator examine and question the standards, or assumptions, by which administrative decisions are made. The standards should reflect to some degree the core values of society though not relying exclusively on custom and tradition. Ethical standards may change as we achieve a better understanding of absolute moral standards.

## The 1970's

For public administration, the culmination of the 1960's period of questioning and challenging traditional roles, institutions, and values was the development of the "New Public Administration" (Marini, 1971). This new tradition represented a changing society and a new environment for public administration. A new interpretation of the responsibilities of administrators was emerging, accompanied by changing values among those administrators.

One New Public Administration scholar argued that a new approach to normative theory in public administration "must accommodate the values and motives of individual public administrators to theories of administrative responsibility" (Harmon, 1971:179). This interpretation reflects a synthesis of the concern of Anderson in the 1950's for focusing on the administrator's "philosophy of personal and social living" (Anderson, 1954:2) with the focus of the 1960's on challenging institutions and the roles of administrators in those institutions. Attention then turned to finding a new normative framework to replace the old.

David K. Hart described the existing ethical framework of public administration as being centered on "impartial administration" and suggested that it "has now outlived its usefulness" (Hart, 1974:4). But rather than calling for detached, scholarly criticism of alternative ethical theories to replace the outdated impartial administration, Hart suggests it is necessary to advocate a specific alternative, so as to provide an immediate replacement for the old paradigm in which public confidence had deteriorated. He argued that "social equity" could serve as a basic operational guideline for public administration (replacing impartial administration in that role) and that "to realize that potential, a theory of social equity must be derived from a carefully explicated ethical paradigm" (Hart, 1974:4). He suggested that John Rawls' *A Theory of Justice* (Rawls, 1971) provides just the "carefully explicated ethical paradigm" that would be necessary to legitimize and operationalize social equity as the new ethical paradigm of public administration. Thus, Hart accommodated the changing values of both society and individual administrators.

In two important ways, the ideas of both Harmon and Hart appear to be consistent with Model III, the framework for understanding administrative ethics as it had developed through the 1960's. First, both questioned standards on which administrative decisions had been made, and second, both suggested that a new moral standard was evolving which was a better reflection of the core values of society.

Nicholas Henry, in his 1975 book *Public Administration and Public Affairs*, similarly described the changing administrative role and its impact on administrative ethics. He pointed out that when public administrators were perceived as mere executors or implementors of policies which they had no role in making, then morality was not a central concern. "Morality, after all, necessitates ethical choice, and, as the literature was wont to stress, ethical choice simply was not a function of the functionaries" (Henry, 1975:33). But, by acknowledging that bureaucrats were involved in the politics of making public policy, this profoundly affected the role of morality in administrative life.

Now the public administrator was forced to make decisions not on the comfortable bases of efficiency, economy, and administrative principles, but on the more agonizing criteria of moral choices as well . . . Public administrationists became increasingly cognizant of the disquieting notion that a sense of ethics—a sense of the public interest—was a genuine need in the practice of public administration. (Henry, 1975:33-34)

What is needed for the public administrator is a simple and operational conceptualization of the public interest that permits him to make a moral choice on the basis of rational thinking. (Henry, 1975:40)

Henry rejects the possibility that administrative responsibility and accountability ensure decision making in the public interest, and also rejects the notion that "radical humanism" (which places human beings as the most important end or goal in all bureaucratic decisions) could provide the framework necessary for making decisions in the public interest. Instead he suggests that John Rawls' "justice as fairness" principles do provide the necessary framework.

Were these scholars attempting to discern a new set of external controls or values which would be uniformly practiced by public administrators? It is not entirely clear. On the one hand, there is a *rejection* of past values such as absolute impartiality which were intended to be uniformly practiced by administrators, and there is some discussion of a replacement for those outmoded practices. But on the other hand, there is at least an *implied* tolerance for individuality among administrators, as reflected in the calls of these same scholars for more open and tolerant organizations, and increased administrative discretion. There is some indication that individuality can legitimately emerge in the practice of administrative ethics, with definitions and interpretations of ethical standards differing among administrators, and changing over time. At the same time, they were reluctant to leave such concepts as "social equity" solely to the interpretation of individuals, thus explaining the efforts to apply Rawls' theory of justice as the "new ethical paradigm."

*Process and Content.* We now return to an issue raised earlier: does being ethical mean first discovering and then applying the expected social standards to administrative decisions? Or does being ethical require that one add another dimension to the above, and actively question and critique the standards which society expects administrators to apply in their decision making? This question illustrates that there are two separate dimensions to ethics, the *content* dimension and the *process* dimension. The distinctions between the two dimensions and the implications of the distinctions are very important to the development of a framework to guide administrative ethics.

The *content* dimension might be described as an explicitly defined set of values (such as Anderson's core values, the social equity values of the new public administration, or the values which might be contained in a code of ethics) which are expected to inform ethical behavior. The *process* dimension might be described as the process of examining, questioning, and deliberating over the values or standards which currently guide administrative action, in order that custom not be relied upon too heavily, and in order that competing or conflicting values might be weighed or debated fairly in reaching a decision. In essence, the content dimension provides a normative statement of the values which are to guide administrative action, while the process dimension provides a procedural approach to questioning those explicit values in order that change might occur, or that the values would be weighed and applied appropriately.

In terms of the literature on public administration ethics already examined, one can see that both the process and content dimensions are addressed, but typically one dimension or the other is emphasized by a particular writer. Leys (1944), for example, was very much concerned with ethics as a *process of thinking* about what standards should be applied to making a decision about a policy matter. He recognized that customs and standard methods of judging policies would not continue to be adequate ethical standards indefinitely. Anderson (1954), on the other hand, sought to establish the core values that should guide administrative action—in other words, identifying the *content* of the ethical standards, which administrators should then apply.

By the 1970's, scholars were challenging the prevailing notions about what standards should inform administrative decisions (i.e., what was to constitute the *content* dimension of ethics) and were suggesting alternative sets of standards. But, as noted above, it is not entirely clear whether authors such as Hart (1974) and Henry (1975) were exclusively concerned with revising the content of ethical standards and then having *all* administrators apply the standards in a uniform fashion, or if some degree of individual interpretation might be appropriate. If such individual interpretation is viewed as acceptable, then being ethical is something more than discovering ethical rules (content dimension) and instead also involves a process dimension in which the individual deliberates over and critiques the standards which are guiding administrative behavior at a particular time.

One possible impetus for focusing on the content dimension might be a desire to exert some control over the behavior of public administrators. Along with the recognition that administrators make significant public policy decisions came the realization that there was somewhat less control over their behavior than would be ideal. If the content of ethical decision standards could be agreed upon, then administrators might be held accountable to those standards.

Defining the content of ethical standards is a particularly difficult task since agreement about that content is hard to come by. For that reason, the *process* of thinking about ethics becomes an important mechanism for reaching decisions in the absence of total agreement on the appropriate *content* of ethical standards. Consider this opinion, expressed by Fritz Morstein Marx in an early article on administrative ethics. "Infinitely more important than compelling administrative officials to live up to minutely defined requirements of control is their acceptance of an ethical obligation to account to themselves and to the public for the *public* character of their actions" (Marx, 1949:1134-1135). Thus, acceptance of a *process* of accountability is more important than defining rules (content) to compel administrators.

Another ethics scholar, James S. Bowman, examined administrative ethics (he used the term "managerial ethics") as a means of addressing the decrease in confidence that the public came to have regarding business and government following scandals such as Watergate. He suggested that since "ethics deals with all forms of managerial behavior . . . it cuts through many of the dimensions of the crisis of confidence today" (Bowman, 1976:48). Following Webster's dictionary he initially defined "ethics" broadly as concerned with "judgments about what is right and wrong and whether or not these judgments are good or bad," perhaps viewing this as the broadest interpretation of ethics. This definition seems quite consistent with Leys' interpretation of ethics as the study of standards (judgments) by which we evaluate administrative decisions and actions.

Bowman followed by defining *ethical conduct* as "that which conforms to professional standards of behavior" (Bowman, 1976:48), and mentions professional accountability, which is a more operational definition for the public administrators to whom it is directed and also a definition which expresses some outside control over administrative behavior. In this context it seems that the author's intent is to give the professional administrator a source for guidance (or content) in defining what his or her ethical responsibilities are. In this case Bowman suggests professional norms, standards, and accountability exert some degree of control over administrative behavior, and might provide some definition of *content* in an otherwise ambiguous *process* of acting ethically.

Treating ethics as only a process could lead to two different but very serious problems. First, administrators may feel paralyzed at the point of making a decision with ethical ramifications because they have had so little guidance as to what morals or values they are expected to follow. Alternatively, administrators may take that lack of specific guidance as *carte blanche* approval of applying their own private value standards to *public* decisions. Each individual administrator is likely to respond to the ambiguity differently, and if the two extremes mentioned above are very common responses, we could find the resulting actions and decisions to be totally unsatisfactory.

Therefore, in consideration of both of those potential problems, writers in the field of administrative ethics often focus a great deal of attention on providing some *content* references or boundaries to inform the ethical standards which administrators are expected to apply. However, those content references are known to change over time, leaving administrators constantly uncertain.

Since there are significant problems associated with emphasis only on process issues, and different but also significant problems associated with emphasis only on content issues, a reasonable conclusion is that some degree of balance must be achieved in addressing *both* dimensions of ethics in arriving at appropriate and workable guidelines for an ethical public administration. In other words, it is important to give administrators some guidance as to what the content of their ethical standards should generally include, but it is equally important to acquaint them with the process of thinking in an ethical manner so that when standards begin to change, or principles don't "fit" the situation, they will be able to act or make a decision in an ethical manner. This leads to a further refinement of the framework:

### Model IV—The 1970's

To be ethical requires that an administrator engage in the process of examining and questioning the standards, or assumptions, by which administrative decisions are made. Standards may need to change over time and the administrator should be able to respond to the new challenges and new demands by updating those standards. The content of the administrator's standards should reflect a commitment to the core values of our society, and the administrator must recognize that he or she will ultimately be held accountable for the standards which inform decisions as well as for the decisions themselves.

Keeping this statement of the operational framework in mind, the two most comprehensive efforts in public administration ethics will be examined, and used to refine the model: John Rohr's *Ethics for Bureaucrats* (1978) and Terry L. Cooper's *The Responsible Administrator* (1982, 1986).

## COMPREHENSIVE TREATMENTS OF PUBLIC ADMINISTRATION ETHICS: ROHR AND COOPER

### Rohr

Early in his book, Rohr differentiates his work on administrative ethics from much of what had come before. There had been a period of time when to be "ethical" meant to avoid bribes, illicit sex, conflicts of interest, and lies. Given scandals such as Watergate, it is not surprising that such issues were paramount in the minds of those writing about the ethical qualities of government officials. However, Rohr's book brought back to our attention the fact that situations in which ethics is a concern are far more commonplace than the periodic scandals would indicate. This reorientation of how we think about public administration ethics is perhaps the most important contribution made by Rohr's book, as it has clearly changed the focus of discussion since that time. Ethically relevant decisions are now recognized as involving questions such as how forcefully to apply equal opportunity policies in hiring, or whether a particular group of people should be provided agency services. These are ethical issues because they involve making a decision based on some moral standard in addition to staying within the guidelines of the law.

Rohr says that he uses the term ethics "in a more general sense than one often finds in contemporary discussions of ethical issues . . . (examining) broader questions of moral character that educators once took more seriously than we do today" (Rohr, 1978:2). He says at a later point in the book that "ethical training and education of the bureaucrat should encourage reflections aimed at developing the virtues we look for in those who govern . . . a keen alertness to the values of those in whose name and for whose benefit one governs" (Rohr, 1978:40). He states that this point of view is necessary because the actions and decisions of bureaucrats inevitably affect the public, and therefore it is the responsibility of bureaucrats to carry out their work in the public interest.

Recalling that Nicholas Henry also linked administrative ethics to a commitment to the public interest we begin to see a pattern emerging which contributes to our understanding of the boundaries within which we can define the *content* of administrative ethics. If we conclude at some point that in order to be ethical, a public administrator must act in the public interest, it excludes at least some modes of thought as to what constitutes being ethical, and starts us on the road to better understanding administrative ethics.

Rohr recognizes that given the many decisions administrators must make in carrying out their work, and the degree of discretionary authority so many administrators have, defining exactly what an administrator should do in any given instance (or defining precisely the standards by which a decision must be made) is quite impossible. At the same time, it is not possible for legislators to write policies in such a way that administrators will never be presented with a situation in which they must interpret and define exactly how the policy is to be implemented. There are too many variables and unique situations for that approach to be reasonable. Therefore, if we are to have administrators making decisions in the public interest, they must be educated in methods of doing so.

Rohr describes three possible approaches to training administrators in the *process* of making ethical decisions. First, he describes the "high road," which is thus labeled because it seems to require the most of those who are to be ethical, both in terms of training and in terms of incorporating ethics into every action and decision they make (Rohr, 1978:55). The high road refers to approaches such as David K. Hart's suggestion that Rawls' principles of justice serve as guidelines for administrators in making ethical decisions. Rohr criticizes this approach because he believes that accepting Rawls' *Theory of Justice* as a starting point for a course in public administration ethics would require that students have more than just the smattering of philosophy which is included in the typical public administration curriculum, and would involve far more time and study than can reasonably be included in the curriculum of a professional course of study (Rohr, 1978:56).

Criticizing the "high road," Rohr views Leys' work as too philosophical to really be of much help to administrators seeking answers to perplexing questions (Rohr, 1978:79n). This seems to be an expression of concern that public administrators would not be able to apply philosophical approaches to administrative decisions, thus making a philosophical approach impractical.

It might be said that Rohr's criticisms of the high road show too little confidence in the ability of students of public administration and too much emphasis on what is necessary to understand and apply the works of Rawls and other philosophers. However, his basic concerns are that administrators truly understand the foundations on which their ethical standards are based, and be able to independently apply the standards. These are certainly important and valuable considerations.

Rohr goes on to describe the "low road" approach to administrative ethics which "addresses ethical issues almost exclusively in terms of adherence to agency rules" (Rohr, 1978:52). Rohr's example of this approach is the U.S. Department of Agriculture's use of a manual designed to train its employees to act in accordance with agency rules even when the rules don't cover a specific situation. For example, one question asks if it is appropriate to use a government car to take one's laundry out to be cleaned while on an official business trip away from home. The issues addressed by this approach have to do with stealing, pilfering, use of official time for personal activities, and so forth.

The "low road" approach is criticized because of "its hopelessly negative approach to public service" (Rohr, 1978:54). The focus is on trivial questions of telephone use while important policy dilemmas are not even acknowledged. The low road is an exercise in internalization of agency rules and becoming the epitome of the stereotyped bureaucrat whose ability to make decisions and to act goes no further than what is explicitly included in agency policy and within the realm of his or her job description. Rohr concludes that the low road approach represents very little progress toward our goal of enabling administrators to make ethical decisions under conditions of policy ambiguity and moral uncertainty. In other words neither the process nor the content dimensions of an adequate framework for administrative ethics has been provided along the low road.

Rohr proposes what he considers to be a "middle road," one which is reasonable to expect of the professional public administrator and public administration program. It is also one which addresses both the content and process dimensions of a system of ethical standards needed by the practicing administrator making significant policy decisions. Since Rohr's "middle road" represents a comprehensive effort to develop an approach to administrative ethics, it will be discussed and critiqued in some detail on the following pages.

Early in the book Rohr establishes that bureaucrats have enough discretionary authority to allow them to govern at times, or to make public policy. In a democratic society, governing is to be done in the name of, in the interests of, and in accordance with the values of the people who are subject to that government. In other words, those who govern must be responsive to the citizens of the nation, or act in the *public interest*. For bureaucrats, this responsiveness is not ensured through periodic elections or reappointment by an elected official. Therefore, bureaucrats must meet this obligation through self-enforced ethical standards. The question Rohr responds to deals with how bureaucrats can and should go about discovering what the values of the citizens are.

Rohr defines values as "beliefs, passions, and principles that have been held for several generations by the overwhelming majority of American people" (Rohr, 1978:65). He states further that "bureaucrats have taken an oath to uphold the Constitution that brought this regime into being and continues to state symbolically its spirit and meaning" (Rohr, 1978:67). Thus, the Constitution is the source to which administrators can look for a list of regime values, which should reflect and illuminate the public interest.

Having a list of values held by the society, however, is insufficient in terms of providing the content dimension of ethics, and insufficient in instructing administrators in the process of making ethical decisions. (Rohr does not use the terms "content dimension" or "process dimension"—these terms are used in interpreting Rohr's work just as they have been used to interpret the work of others.) The interpretations of the values to be found in the Constitution are as varied as the interpreters. Thus, Rohr explains, instructing bureaucrats or administrators to turn to the Constitution as their guide in defining the public interest and providing a content dimension to their ethical deliberation is about the same as asking that they exclusively allow their personal morals to inform their decisions.

In order to provide more substantive content for abstract values such as freedom and equality, Rohr suggests turning to opinions found in Supreme Court cases which have focused on the values in question. The dialectic established by the opinions in each case, including concurring and dissenting opinions, will help to better inform the ethical choice, "and thereby help them avoid the danger of accepting dogmatic assertions uncritically" (Rohr, 1978:70). This is proposed by Rohr as a tool in the professional education of administrators and as a technique which might be used occasionally by a practicing administrator, although not on a daily basis, as it would be too time-consuming.

Given the above summary of Rohr's work, it appears that he addresses both the content dimension of ethics (by defining the

Constitution as a reference for regime values) and the process dimension of ethics (through his suggestions about exploring the views proposed in the Supreme Court decisions as a guide to informed and ethical administrative decisions.) He also emphasizes the broad decision-making authority of administrators, and thus the extensive need for ethical deliberation. All this seems in keeping with the operational framework that developed through the 1970's. Indeed, Rohr's book might be thought of as the definitive work on public administration ethics as it had developed up to that point. Even so, there are some criticisms of Rohr's regime values model, possibly indicating that the proposed model or framework for administrative ethics is not yet fully developed. Three criticisms of Rohr's regime values approach to administrative ethics will be presented, then the theoretical model will be refined to incorporate the observations made.

First, referring to Rohr's own examples of the discretionary decisions which must be made by administrators (Rohr, 1978:34–37), it is clear that administrators are in need of ethical standards that they can use and apply on a daily basis—not just when time and inclination permit. Examining Supreme Court decisions is probably a useful tool in training administrators, but would fall short of what they need in actual practice because applying the values to particular cases would be difficult and too time-consuming for regular use.

Secondly, Supreme Court decisions, by their very nature, deal with issues of the past and cannot always be expected to give the kind of guidance an administrator needs in trying to determine the content of the ethical standards of today. Nor would the cases always be of much help in anticipating changes in our ethical standards. In other words, relying on Supreme Court decisions to inform us about the content of the regime values may very well lock us into custom and tradition in a way that Leys in the 1940's recognized as inadequate in a rapidly changing world.

Finally, and again referring to concerns raised by Leys, reliance upon Supreme Court decisions does not help administrators to overcome the "feeling of presumptiveness and hesitancy whenever you undertake to evaluate things in the name of your own judgment" (Leys, 1944:12). It would seem much more appropriate to train administrators to rely more often on their own judgment in making the daily decisions in the public interest (or according to society's core values). This would require that attention be focussed on providing the necessary training and socialization to enable administrators to make those judgments independently, yet still in a manner consistent with regime values and the public interest.

Rather than internalizing agency rules as suggested in the "low road" approach, administrators might be expected to internalize and operationalize society's values as expressed in the Constitution and elsewhere. This is probably not the difficult task that it at first appears to be. Persons who have been socialized in this country probably share most, if not all, of the regime values to one degree or another. The process of becoming informed about and understanding the social values in question is probably just a matter of raising to a conscious and working level beliefs already held by most members of society. Anderson suggested something very similar to this in his 1953 speech.

If administrators could incorporate societal values into their decision making with some degree of confidence and accuracy, it would not be necessary to search for a precedent in Supreme Court opinions in order to justify a decision. An administrator must always be able to justify decisions, but it would be more appropriate for the administrator to *personally* develop the justification (in terms of social values) rather than resorting to seeking out a justification in the text of Supreme Court opinions. The task would be less tedious, more appropriate to the situation, and also more consistent with efforts to have administrators make *all* decisions in an ethical manner.

In order to accomplish this last goal, an administrator must be able to apply the process and content dimensions of ethics without being encumbered by methods that require too much time or continuous reliance on the thinking of others (e.g., Supreme Court justices). A reasonable goal for any framework of ethics would be to prepare administrators to make ethical decisions somewhat independently. This will be possible only if there has been significant guidance in the process and content frameworks somewhere early in the training or career of an administrator, and at the same time sufficient avenues of accountability so that the public can confidently allow administrators the authority to make those judgments when necessary.

So, though Rohr's work contributes a great deal to the development of public administration ethics, one aspect of an ideal approach to administrative ethics does seem to be lacking. That is a semblance of *independence* for the administrator in carrying out ethical deliberations and making ethical decisions on a daily basis. This added dimension leads to a refinement of the concept of "being ethical" as follows:

## Model V—After Rohr

To be ethical requires that an administrator be able to independently engage in the process of reasonably examining and questioning the standards by which administrative decisions are made. The content of the standards may change over time as social values are better understood, or new social concerns are expressed. An administrator should be ready to adapt decision standards to these changes, always reflecting a commitment to the core values of our society. The administrator must recognize that he or she will be held personally and professionally accountable for the decisions made and for the ethical standards which inform those decisions.

It is important to note here that Rohr's views about the Constitution and public administration go considerably beyond the particular role of Supreme Court decisions focused on before. He continued his study of this area in a later book, *To Run a Constitution*, in which he proposed a normative theory "intended to encourage administrators and the public to think about administrative behavior in constitutional terms" (Rohr, 1986b:182-183). He suggested also that the role of Public Administration is to uphold "the Constitution . . . (and) that administrators should use their discretionary power in order to maintain the constitutional balance of powers in support of individual rights" (Rohr, 1986b:181). His is a provocative argument sufficiently persuasive that any administrative ethics curriculum that neglects the Constitutional foundation is lacking a very important dimension.

### Cooper

A second comprehensive treatment of ethics in the public sector is Terry L. Cooper's *The Responsible Administrator* (1982). Cooper reports that the ultimate purpose of his book is to "illuminate the ethical situation of the public administrator and cultivate imaginative reflection about it, not to prescribe a particular set of public service values," and that there is "no attempt . . . to engage in the development of a substantive ethic for public administrators" (Cooper, 1982:7). Thus his focus is mainly on the process dimension of ethics rather than on the content dimension.

Cooper differentiates his work from Rohr's by commenting that Rohr's work "does structure the search for administrative ethics along realistic and manageable lines," but that the missing dimension of Rohr's book is "the process of ethical decision making" (Cooper, 1982:8). Cooper argues that Supreme Court opinions might lead an administrator to the appropriate regime values for the circumstances, but that applying those values becomes much more complicated when one considers the environment and circumstances in which administrators are making and carrying out decisions.

"Ethics involves substantive reasoning about obligations, consequences, and ultimate ends," Cooper argues (Cooper, 1982:4), and "doing ethics . . . involves thinking more systematically about values which are embedded in the choices we make" (Cooper, 1982:13). He indicates that the process of being ethical ultimately requires the individual administrator to apply those values and make a decision, though Cooper makes little effort to define those appropriate values or decision standards. Ultimately he emphasizes the need to improve control over the decisions of individual administrators.

The last half of Cooper's book is devoted to exploring methods of maintaining the responsible conduct of individual administrators making individual decisions about the ordering of social values. Cooper attempts to ensure that some control would be exerted over the individual administrator even in the absence of a "substantive ethic" (the term Cooper uses to indicate the content dimension of the ethical framework). In other words, he is attempting to develop a process dimension that provides guidelines for administrators as to their various responsibilities as well as accountability and control dimensions. Essentially Cooper outlines the roles, responsibilities, and obligations of administrators which, he says, should serve as boundaries in the process of ethical decision making. Within those boundaries, a substantive (content) dimension of ethics can be applied. Cooper conceives of the ethical administrator as one who adheres to organizational responsibilities and roles, while applying appropriate ethical standards to administrative decisions.

Thus, the *organization*, for the first time is being fully developed as an important component of the ethical process—a component that places new demands and new constraints on administrative behavior. Basic to the understanding of how organizations can become a part of the ethical process is a "recognition that real power is held by persons at various levels of an organization" and that individual power "can be held accountable only if it is recognized, identified, sanctioned and bounded" (Cooper, 1982:132).

Cooper suggests that if administrators know what decisions are legitimately theirs to make, have representation and participation in the policy-making process, and have a clear understanding of the goals of the organization, their decisions can be bounded and they can be held accountable. Without lines of accountability, the public and organizational superiors would be reluctant to accept the administrator's power as legitimate. In addition, since organizational obligations and constraints are a very real dimension of the practice of public administration, failure to take them into account will result in a much weaker theoretical model for administrative ethics.

In the second edition of his book, Cooper more fully develops his analysis of the relationship between the administrator, the organization, and ethics, emphasizing the "fundamental importance of the organizational environment for individual ethical decision making" (Cooper, 1986:x). He points out that too often public administrators "have little ethical autonomy because they allow the organizations that employ them too much importance in the overall pattern of their lives" (Cooper, 1986:xvii), and he outlines ways in which administrators can transcend that organizational influence while at the same time operating within the necessary constraints of organizational life.

Cooper's work thus suggests a crucial refinement to the model of ethical action:

### Model VI—After Cooper

To be ethical requires that an administrator be able to independently engage in the process of reasonably examining and questioning the standards by which administrative decisions are made, at least to the extent that the decisions are legitimately made at that level of the organization. The content of the standards may change over time as social values are better understood, or new social concerns are expressed. An administrator should be ready to adapt decision standards to these changes, always reflecting a commitment to the core values of our society and recognition of the goals of the organization. The administrator will be held accountable personally, professionally, and within the organization for the decisions made and for the ethical standards which inform those decisions.

This lengthy definition of ethical administration may be somewhat imposing on first look. It can be restated as: administrative ethics is a process of independently critiquing decision standards, based on core social values which can be discovered, within reasonable organizational boundaries which can be defined, subject to personal and professional accountability. One major advantage of this model is that those who are affected by the administrative decisions have some control over the process in that there are lines of authority and systems of accountability which can serve as a check on administrative behavior, while still allowing the necessary individual discretion for ethical conduct.

This model of administrative ethics reflects the development of thinking within the discipline of public administration, but requires further review and refinement. Specifically, the philosophical traditions of ethics and political thought are both important in the development of a sound theoretical framework and in testing the legitimacy of such a framework. While it is beyond the scope of this particular book to fully explore those philosophical traditions, at least a sampling of that literature would be beneficial in critiquing and refining the framework, and perhaps more importantly, establishing the need for further exploration of this heritage.

## THE PHILOSOPHICAL TRADITION OF ETHICS

There are three major aspects of the previously developed framework which will be discussed in terms of definitions of ethics from the philosophical literature. Those three aspects are:

1. Ethical action involves a process of examining and questioning accepted standards for making decisions, a process which must at times be carried out independently. (*Independent critique*)
2. The content of the ethical standards should reflect the core values of society and that the understanding of those values can, and will, change over time, thus changing the standards by which actions are to be evaluated. (*Changing standards*)
3. Administrators, because they are not only acting as individuals but also as members of an organization, must consider their role within the organization and the goals of the organization as part of a determination of how to act or standards to use in making decisions. (*Organizational context*)

Each of these components will be examined in light of selections from the philosophical traditions of ethics and political thought. One objective is to find possible inconsistencies between the operational model of administrative ethics and ethical models from other philosophical traditions. A second objective is to begin to explore how the philosophical traditions can be more extensively applied in both the research and practice of administrative ethics.

### Independent Critique and Changing Standards

Since the logical end product of independent critique is that standards can change or come to be understood differently, these two aspects will be explored together. The *Encyclopedia of Philosophy* (1967) states that the term "ethics" is "used in three different but related ways, signifying (1) a general pattern or 'way of life,' (2) a set of rules of conduct or 'moral code,' and (3) inquiry *about* ways of life and rules of conduct" (Abelson and Nielson, 1967:81-82). The first use of the term refers to Buddhist or Judeo-Christian ethics, the second refers to the concept of a code, as one might find in professional ethics. The third refers to a branch of philosophy (metaethics) (Abelson and Nielson, 1967:82). The usages are related in that they each assume the discoverability of right rules of conduct which should guide behavior, and assume that one ought to follow those rules of conduct. In the case of the second use (professional ethics) those rules are assumed to be known. In the case of the third usage (the branch of philosophy), the rules are assumed to be open to further inquiry and discussion. If the rules of right conduct are assumed to be known, then they can be referred to as the content dimension of ethics. If the rules of right conduct are still open to further inquiry and discovery, they then might indicate that there is a process (of inquiry) dimension to ethics, involving the study and critique of the right rules of conduct as they are currently practiced. This parallels with the dimensions of public administration ethics discussed earlier.

Richard B. Brandt defines ethical theory as "a body of reflection answering, or intended to answer, certain questions about ethical statements" (statements about what is desirable or morally obligatory) (Brandt, 1959:1-2). He distinguishes two branches of ethical theory: "normative ethics, which deals with the questions of 'Which ethical statements are true or valid?' and 'Why?'," and critical ethics, which "deals with the problem of justifying and the problem of analyzing the meaning and function of ethical statements" (Brandt, 1959:4-8). Ethics as the term has been used in the administrative ethics model most closely resembles Brandt's normative ethics in that it involves a search for ethical statements which are true and valid and which can guide behavior in making administrative decisions.

Brandt goes on to say that normative ethics "is not only the formulation of valid ethical principles, whether very abstract and general or relatively concrete, but also a defense or justification of accepting these principles" (Brandt, 1959:7). He also mentions that some departments of social sciences draw on ethical theory for the "critique and justification of institutions" (Brandt, 1959:12). Brandt recognizes that normative ethics is limited because "it can hardly be expected to provide a list of basic ethical principles that will be acceptable to all persons . . . perhaps the most important thing we have to gain from the tradition of ethical theory is a *model* for an ethical system . . . then we must criticize our own system of ethical principles" (Brandt, 1959:14).

Brandt's work lends credence to the view held in some of the public administration ethics literature that the process of being ethical requires critique of the standards by which decisions are made (i.e., critique and deliberation over the currently accepted standards or *content*). In other words, a model for the content of public administration ethics might be provided, but the model must be subject to a continuous process of inquiry and deliberation as it is used to guide administrative action, thus legitimizing both independent critique and the possibility of changing standards.

Simone de Beauvoir, in *The Ethics of Ambiguity*, states that "ethics does not furnish recipes any more than do science and art. One can merely propose methods" (de Beauvoir, 1948:134). Certainly, the *process* dimension of administrative ethics is an effort to propose a method or model by which ethical judgments can be made, and the developing framework for administrative ethics moved in that direction for very much the same reason that de Beauvoir gave: there were no agreed-upon recipes for administrative ethics, so it was necessary to develop methods or processes of ethical decision making instead.

Finally, A. Campbell Garnett in *Ethics: A Critical Introduction* states that "critical examination of accepted ethical judgments is therefore a constant requirement in every progressive social order. This does not imply any lack of respect for accepted ethical principles. It implies only a recognition that accepted principles are not necessarily the best and that it is very important that we should know what principles are best and accept them." He then gives a second reason for the study of ethics: "to develop independence and individual strength of character"

(Garnett, 1960:5-6). If ours is assumed to be a "progressive social order," then Garnett's view that critical examination of ethical principles is a necessary part of being progressive would again support the critical or questioning component of ethical administration.

Garnett's second reason for the study of ethics adds a new dimension. We might recall that one of the "core values" mentioned by Hurst Anderson was the significance of the individual human personality (Anderson, 1954:4). If critically examining decision standards develops the individual moral character of the administrator, this is an outcome worth valuing in itself.

In political philosophy one will also find a concern about the notion of independent critique and changing ethical standards. For example, Plato thought in terms of Forms which "one can discover through reason, observation, and dialectic" (Sibley, 1970:68-69) and which the Rulers of the ideal republic are charged with contemplating and applying "to the function of coordination and governance" (Sibley, 1970:71). This would support both the contention that critique (through contemplation) is not only allowable, but desirable, and that through time the Forms will come to be better understood through these efforts.

While Plato reserved this contemplative/critique function to an elite group who must make laws and govern the republic, Aristotle recognized that "there is however another crucial link between virtues and law, for knowing how to apply the law is itself possible only for someone who possesses the virtue of justice" (MacIntyre, 1984:152). Thus, making the laws or rules will be insufficient. Knowing how to apply those laws—the administrative task—requires good judgment and the application of virtues. So the philosophy of Aristotle also lends support to the administrative ethics model in which administrators make judgments independently, applying and exhibiting a well developed, virtuous character.

*Ethics, Values, and Morality.* When discussing "independent critique" and "changing standards" it is impossible to avoid the problem of terminology. The terms ethics, values, and morality are frequently used interchangeably or at least not clearly distinguished from one another. This is in part true because "moral" and "ethical" are in many ways synonymous, since they are derived from corresponding Latin and Greek words. Modern usage might distinguish the two in that "ethics" has become associated with both philosophical inquiry and professional standards, while morals continue to hold the connotation of "right rules of conduct." For public administration ethics, to be ethical often means to follow right rules of moral conduct, but being ethical can also legitimately mean to be engaged in the inquiry into what those right rules of moral conduct are or should be, or how they might be applied when two or more right rules of conduct conflict.

One aspect of the administrative ethics model which it might be useful to review, then, is that part which states that the content of our ethical standards should reflect the core values of our society, given a dynamic and changing understanding of those core values over time. The term "core values" was used because that is what Hurst Anderson (1954) called the list of spiritual and moral values which he wrote about. Golembiewski referred to the term "morals" as the "absolute standards which exist beyond time" (Golembiewski, 1965:61). This raises the question as to whether "values" or "morals" is the more appropriate term to use when referring to those absolute standards which are a part of the fabric of our society, even if not the practical norm at any given time.

Kurt Baier, philosopher and author of *The Moral Point of View: A Rational Basis of Ethics*, defines morality as "a certain part of the system of reasons (for or against entering on certain lines of action) acknowledged as overriding" (Baier, 1965:xix). Later he explained that morality is also "a body of rules or precepts for which there are certain tests . . . morality is a comparatively sophisticated system of rules, and we have to admit the possibility of nonmoral or premoral societies" (Baier, 1965:89). While we may choose to leave to philosophers the task of determining whether our body of rules or precepts meets those "tests," still it would be valuable to discover the rules and precepts that our society acknowledges as overriding. Anderson may have begun this process for us by listing the core values, and Rohr may have carried it further in his discussion of regime values. Mortimer Adler also contributed to that understanding in his book *Six Great Ideas* (1981), where he explored liberty, equality, justice, truth, goodness, and beauty as the central ideas of our society. In any event, in Baier's terms "morality" may be a more appropriate term for what we had called "core values," because morality implies a more lasting and overriding perspective than would "values" which seems to refer to something more temporary in nature and more open to disagreement among individuals.

Richard Means in *The Ethical Imperative* distinguishes between values and ethics, terms he says are intimately related but not the same thing. "Ethics are the normative standards of conduct derived from the philosophical and religious traditions of society" (Means, 1969:55). Values, on the other hand, are norms which underlie rational social action and which change over time. "The philosophers of Western ethics generally agree that the linguistic form to express ethical injunctions is 'ought to' while values are expressed in the 'is' form" (Means, 1969:55).

Following on the "is/ought to" distinction, we can find support for Means' contention in the political thought of Thomas Acquinas. Acquinas saw the possibility that human laws might be unjust by being contrary to the common good or in some other way violating natural law, and thus would be non-binding (Sibley, 1970: 235-243). "Human law" then would be the "is," while "natural law" would be the "ought to be" toward which we should strive.

Means' definition of the term "ethics" seems more closely related to what Anderson meant by "core values" than does Means' definition of values—there was clearly an "ought to" dimension in Anderson's work and that of most writers in the field of administrative ethics. For that reason, it seems advisable to change the terminology of our model of ethical action, deleting reference to "core values" and referring instead to either the "ethic" or, preferably, the "morality" or "moral order" of our society as Golembiewski and Baier use the terms. This seems much more consistent with what it means to be ethical than using a term (value) which indicates a perspective based only on what presently "is."

Another dimension of the changing nature of social morality is the question of whether the morality itself is changing, or just our understanding of that morality. Donaldson and Werhane (1983) point out that a relativistic basis of moral obligation is based on time, place, and circumstance, while in an absolutist basis of moral obligation there is a universal code which is only in the process of discovery (Donaldson and Werhane, 1983:35).

It is not necessary to resolve here the debate between the relativists and the absolutists (though this will be taken up again in Chapter 2). In either case, administrators will be faced with a changing definition of moral obligation either because time and circumstance change, or because of a more highly developed understanding of the universal code. In either case, the obligations of the administrator must be recognized, and decision standards changed accordingly. The results of conscientiously seeking to understand the morality of our society may be as Means said: "If we gave more attention to the sources and variety of value traditions, we would become better attuned to society's problems. Our perceptions of the social problems of our day can be no better than the standards of our ethics" (Means, 1969:263).

## Organizational Context

Finally we must consider our view that the administrator's position within the organization should to some extent determine what decisions and actions are appropriate, and how the administrator might be held accountable for those actions. Is this view consistent with the treatment of ethical action in the discipline of ethics? After having emphasized the importance of the individual administrator engaging in critique of the standards by which decisions are made and judged, it seems somewhat inconsistent that it should now be tempered by requiring that the administrator be cognizant of, and constrained by, the organizational role.

Richard Brandt's work may be of some help in establishing a philosophical reason for the importance of giving special consideration to the goals of the organization, and the administrator's role in the organization. He presents an argument in which he concludes that "in general . . . there is a presumption that any generally accepted moral conviction has some validity to it. . . . The accepted moral convictions of one's group are certainly *importantly relevant*; they are likely to be sufficiently defensible so that serious consideration should be given to them" (Brandt, 1959:58). If we view "obedience to legitimate authority" as a generally accepted moral conviction, then that might be an "importantly relevant" consideration for administrators who are contemplating a decision which is in conflict with instructions from a superior in the hierarchy of the organization. This doesn't necessarily mean that the administrator would never question the authority or the goals of the organization, only that there are "importantly relevant" reasons for compliance to authority which should be given special consideration.

Sibley's analysis of Thomas Aquinas' thinking indicates that, while it is possible to have unjust laws, Aquinas is not "certain as to who makes the decision on the justice or injustice of a particular law . . . He does, however, make it clear that even an unjust law should perhaps . . . be obeyed if disobedience would provoke scandal or disturbance" (Sibley, 1970:242).

Perhaps a more compelling reason for giving special consideration to the limits placed on the administrator by the organization is given by Kurt Baier. He discusses the process of deliberation as it applies to choosing among the possible courses of action available to an individual. He states that "the best course of action is not that course which most quickly, least painfully, least expensively, etc., leads to the gaining of our ends, but *it is the course of action which is supported by the best reasons*" (Baier, 1965:28). He goes on to discuss in his book the many possible reasons for choosing a particular alternative, and how individuals may go about weighing the reasons and arriving at a decision.

One of the reasons discussed by Baier is particularly relevant to the problems faced by an administrator when the organizational role seems to require decisions or actions which are morally questionable for the administrator. Baier says that "not the least important contribution which the existence of a society makes to the life that is worth living is the provision of established patterns of behavior giving everyone confidence and security. It provides institutions and definite rules for the realization of the most fundamental human needs and desires"

(Baier, 1965:12). He is suggesting that one reason which might be given for adhering to the established rules and procedures spelled out by the organization is that it gives fellow members of the organization, and the public, confidence and security that they can anticipate the behavior of the administrator. Without such security life would be chaotic, or as Baier says, less "worth living."

This is not to say, however, that administrators must never step beyond the realm of their authority or question organizational rules and goals. It only suggests that there is a special reason for giving strong consideration to the value of doing what people *expect* the administrator to do (such as following direct orders from a superior). This special reason could be sufficiently compelling that the administrator would choose to act in a way that doesn't seem to be the most desirable in that particular case, but more desirable than decreasing the confidence and security of the other members of the organization and the public.

Another political thinker, Peter Singer, argues in *Democracy & Disobedience* that there are good reasons for not disobeying a legitimately arrived-at democratic law. The central reason is that democracy is "a procedure for resolving disputes which depends for its existence on the disputants regarding the verdict of the decision-procedure as having substantial, though not overriding, moral weight because it is the result of the decision-procedure," to which members of the society agreed (Singer, 1974:103-104). Organizational structures and lines of authority might also be thought of as decision procedures to which organizational members and society in general have agreed, and which must therefore have "substantial, though not overriding, moral weight" and should not be challenged lightly by administrators.

This brief sampling of the philosophical tradition of ethics and political thought helps to support the model of ethical administration as a theoretically valid one, with the exception that use of the term "core values" might be misleading and that instead the "morality" of society might be a better term. This implies that there are ultimate standards in our society, though at any given time the norms in practice may not be entirely consistent with that morality. The process of being ethical is an effort to better understand not only the standards by which we act, but also the morality of the society. As a part of the ongoing development of a more ethical public administration there might be a movement toward greater convergence between our ethical standards in practice and the true moral standards of the society.

Perhaps more importantly, using selections from the philosophical traditions of ethics to critique the framework for administrative ethics shows how much those traditions can contribute to a thoughtful dialogue about various aspects of administrative ethics. Unfortunately those traditions are not typically a part of such a discussion.

Though the model of ethical administration that has been developed is a combination of many of the views from the public administration ethics literature, and also appears to be consistent with philosophical approaches to ethics, it is nevertheless a *theoretical* model. As mentioned early in this chapter, no model of ethical action will be very helpful if it cannot be put into practice by administrators. Whether or not the model can meet the test of practicability will be determined as various aspects of the administrator's environment are explored in the following chapters.

# 2

# THE SOCIAL AND HISTORICAL CONTEXT OF PUBLIC ADMINISTRATION

G. W. F. Hegel said the Universal History "is the exhibition of Spirit [the rational and necessitated will of God] in the process of working out the knowledge of that which it is potentially" (Hegel, 1956:17-18). In the same discussion he likened history to the seed of a tree: "As the germ bears in itself the whole nature of the tree, and the taste and form of its fruits, so do the first traces of Spirit virtually contain the whole of that History" (Hegel, 1956:18). Applied to the field of administrative ethics, this philosophy of history would suggest that the diverse contributions to the topic which have been made over time must contain traces of the "whole," or spirit of administrative ethics. But to develop that spirit requires an effort to work out the knowledge of "that which it is potentially."

The conceptual framework developed in the previous chapter contributes to that knowledge, but the effort to fully understand the potential of administrative ethics requires a more thorough examination of the obligations, responsibilities, roles, and influences on administrative practice as these have been seen over time. In other words, the broader context of public administration must be examined for what it contributes to our knowledge of administrative ethics.

The following two chapters will provide the reader with a context within which to carry out an examination of the dynamic and changing field of public administration ethics, as well as providing some insight into the *practice* of administrative ethics. The objective of this chapter is to examine the *social and historical* context of public administration, while Chapter 3 examines the *organizational* context of public administration. Each of these contexts must be accommodated in any theoretically sound and practicable approach to administrative ethics.

The discussion of the social and historical context of public administration will be divided into three parts: (1) The fundamental moral order of the society as it has been understood and as it could be understood; (2) The role of public administration in that moral order and in society; and (3) Our philosophical traditions that suggest approaches for resolving (or at least dealing with) the ambiguities and conflicts identified in the first two sections.

The rationale for this particular approach is that any discussion of ethics must be grounded in some understanding of a moral order. Recall from Chapter 1 that the moral order is the set of rules which society acknowledges as overriding in arguing for or against a course of action. The moral order also provides the basis for critiquing what is currently being defined as ethical, what has become standard practice. Once the moral order is understood to some degree, then it is possible to discuss the administrative role in furthering, protecting, or acting according to that moral order. The moral order, then, serves as the basis for developing the *content* dimension of administrative ethics because it provides the normative foundation on which any notion of ethics must develop. The role of the administrator in relation to other social and political actors helps to define some of the *process* dimensions of administrative ethics in that it outlines some ways of institutionalizing procedures for resolving problems.

Finally, there will be inherent conflicts and unresolved questions in any discussion of public morality and administrative ethics. Therefore, the methods used in structuring or guiding the resolution of those ambiguities are important to the field of administrative ethics. The final section of the chapter will examine how our philosophical traditions can contribute to the understanding of administrative ethics, to the resolution of the ambiguities, and how those traditions have influenced the history of administrative ethics.

## THE MORAL ORDER OF OUR SOCIETY

The nature of values is not static, and values change through time. Only a sense of the moral order coupled with a sense of time can give us the right perspective for identifying social problems. (Means, 1969:26)

Only by maintaining a focus on the moral order (instead of current value structures, or current ethical problems and expectations for administrators) can the field of administrative ethics maintain a perspective that avoids the dangers of accepting current practice as the working definition of the way things "ought to be." Just as "neutral competence" and "social equity" have both gained and lost legitimacy over a period of time, so too will all other narrow interpretations of ethical expectations for administrators. Therefore, it is the lasting moral order that provides the needed perspective for dealing with ethical problems.

The previous sentence states a view that is in marked contrast to John Dewey's pragmatic theory of ethics, which has been influential in the development of American political thought and practice. Dewey's pragmatic view is that out of changing human needs and conditions we develop a new set of values that are instrumental in achieving our desired ends (thus, his theory is often referred to as "instrumentalism"). The desired ends, though, are not intrinsically valuable (or good); they are instead socially constructed and will change as people and circumstance change (Gouinlock, 1976:176-187). Dewey argues that the "conception of what is good must undergo change as society changes and . . . the discrepancy between stated ideals and actual behavior in contemporary society can be understood as due in part to the persistence of obsolete values" (Albert et al., 1969:283). "Dewey attributes the lag of morality behind technology to the effect of the traditional conception of man as a passive spectator in a fixed and unchanging universe, where truth is absolute and eternal" (Albert et al., 1969:281).

Dewey suggests that "only the use of the methods of science in ethics can secure the continuing adaptation of values to changing human needs" and "truth is relative rather than absolute" (Albert et al., 1969:282-283). The assumption of ethical relativism on which Dewey's view is based can be explained as follows: "in the case of basic ethical judgments, there is no objectively valid, rational way of justifying one against another" (Frankena, 1973:109). Therefore, Dewey concludes that as social needs and conditions change, values should be changed in an accommodative fashion.

Dewey's instrumentalism and the theoretical framework for administrative ethics developed in Chapter 1 both view values as transitory, but they differ in a very important way. Dewey's instrumentalism assumes that values should adapt to changing human conditions. The viewpoint adopted in the ethical framework, and implicit in Means' quotation above, is that values should reflect a *reconciliation* of changing human needs with the lasting and fundamental moral order (universal law). These differences are illustrated in Figure 2.1.

If a framework for administrative ethics is built upon relativism and other instrumental assumptions, then as changes in technology and circumstance occur, administrators can assume that ethics or values must change accordingly. If we allow that values are relative, then no serious system of administrative ethics can ever be developed, because it will change as rapidly as technology, leadership, and environments change.

On the other hand, if public administration ethics is based on the notion of a lasting moral order, then new circumstances and technologies will be judged according to that moral order rather than immediately assuming the technology to be moral and ethical and abandoning the moral order. When morality does lag behind technology, or there is a discrepancy between stated ideals and actual behavior, this may well reflect the failure of people to take the difficult route of putting into practice

**Figure 2.1**
**Change and the Moral Order**

| | NATURE OF THE MORAL ORDER | CHANGE IN THE MORAL ORDER |
|---|---|---|
| **INSTRUMENTALISM** | Relative | Moral order changes to accommodate social change |
| **UNIVERSAL LAW** | Absolute | A more comprehensive understanding of the moral order is attained as it is applied in new social settings |

what they very fervently believe. Or, it may reflect the difficulty of knowing how to apply moral principles to rapidly developing technologies which are not yet fully understood. When social values adapt to changing conditions, this may reflect a new understanding of the moral order, not an abandonment of old truths. Thus, truth may well be absolute and unchanging (a view which Dewey lamented) but our understanding and application of the "truth" will remain dynamic, evolving and changing over time.

Reference to "a sense of time" in Means' quotation at the beginning of this section can be interpreted as an indication that the practiced values of our time should be taken into consideration in ethical deliberation, but balanced with "a sense of the moral order." A sense of time without a sense of the moral order can lead administrators to act in a manner consistent with current norms, but which might be judged ultimately as morally reprehensible. Without a sense of time, though, an administrator might act in a manner that fails to reflect the current understanding or interpretation of the moral order, or changes in circumstance or technology which must be considered, critiqued, or accommodated by the moral order. For example, the sanctity of human life is an accepted part of the moral order. How genetic engineering, the ability to freeze embryos, and similar technological developments should be viewed in this regard is problematic. Dewey might argue that our values regarding human life should change to accommodate our new capabilities. Those viewing the sanctity of human life as a universal law might argue that we must carefully examine what we mean by human life, and then judge the new technologies according ⌐ that new understanding. Then the technology (not the moral ᴜᵣder) should be accepted or rejected accordingly.

The notion of a moral order based on universal law has clearly been represented in public administration literature. For example, Dwight Waldo refers to the concept of "higher law" which "holds that there is a source and measure of rightness that is above and beyond both individual and government" (Waldo, 1980:101). The framework of administrative ethics proposed in the previous chapter requires that the moral order that exists beyond time be the morality followed by the ethical administrator. In order to follow that moral order, though, it must be better understood and further defined.

Waldo states that there is no comprehensive and systematic treatise on ethical behavior in public administration, perhaps because "a systematic treatise is impossible, given the scope, complexity, and intractability of the material from which it would have to be constructed and given an inability to find acceptable or defensible foundations of ideas and beliefs on which it could be grounded" (Waldo, 1980:100). The scope and complexity of the material should not be underestimated since it involves the foundations of a society, the rationale for a government, the nature of the individual, moral philosophy, and organization theory, to name only a few of the fields involved.

Nevertheless, to accept as given an "inability to find acceptable or defensible foundations of ideas and beliefs" on which to ground public administration ethics is overly pessimistic. To accept such an inability to provide defensible *content* in administrative ethics leaves us with no choice but to accept the alternative—ethics based upon a relativistic notion of morality which has already been argued to be inadequate.

Clearly, a systematic foundation of ideas and beliefs has not been fully developed and accepted in the field, but not necessarily because it is impossible to do so. Many writers have attempted to define such a foundation. Mortimer Adler, for example, suggests in *Six Great Ideas* (1981) that truth, goodness, and beauty are ideas we judge by, and liberty, equality, and justice are ideas we act on. He explores many of the discussions about those ideas throughout Western thought, and provides insight into those ideas which could certainly be valuable to the development of administrative ethics.

These are other sets of universal laws or rules which have been argued to be present in all or nearly all moral orders, including our own:

respect for the lives of members of the society; respect for truth; respect for cooperation; helpfulness (DeGeorge, 1978)

It is wrong to: misuse social institutions, steal, commit adultery, break promises, neglect duties, or fail to discharge obligations (Baier, 1965)

Individual autonomy and equality; freedom from unwarranted interference; self-respect; the right to security in expectations (Goldman, 1980)

Thus we see that there are some sources of guidance about what might constitute a universal moral order, and some possibility that these ideas could be developed as a defensible and acceptable foundation for administrative ethics.

Even where there is some general agreement about the ideas and beliefs relevant to the moral order, disagreements will arise. These disagreements are indicative of the different interpretations and applications of that moral order arrived at by diverse groups. It would be unrealistic to expect certainty and perfect agreement about the moral order. But to say it is impossible to agree on a basic foundation leaves administrators without any specific moral guidance at all, and free to operate as if in a state of amorality.

If we view the disagreements differently (as contributing to the further refinement of our basic agreement about the foundations of the moral order) then the administrator is provided with some broad guidelines for behavior. The latter interpretation will be argued here to be more appropriate for building a theoretical and practical framework for administrative ethics.

To further explore these issues—instrumentalism, universal laws, the existence of an agreed-upon moral order—and to understand their implications for administrative ethics, it is necessary to turn to moral philosophy, where the debate on these issues has been fully developed, and critiques and defenses of various theories widely explored.

In the field of moral philosophy, there are two general approaches to understanding or thinking about the moral order: a *deontological* approach which focuses on universal rules that serve as guides for moral action and provide good reasons for making a decision; or a *teleological* approach which focuses on the consequences of actions as the determining factor of whether the actions are good or bad. The basic distinction between the two approaches is that one judges the morality of the act by the reasons for the act (a deontological approach) and the other judges morality by the outcomes or consequences of the act (a teleological approach).

These two approaches to understanding the moral order are important to the study of administrative ethics because the way one thinks about the moral order determines what one considers ethical, and how one makes judgments about actions. In addition, the differences between the deontological and teleological approaches explain some of the different stances exhibited in ethical debates, though the debates are rarely couched in these philosophical terms. Therefore, each approach will be examined, followed by a discussion of its application to administrative ethics.

### Deontology: Universal Rules

A deontological approach to understanding the moral order assumes the existence of universally applicable moral principles. Even though the moral principles might not be fully comprehended, people are obligated to try their best to understand and abide by those principles. The moral principles will provide adequate guidance in practice by serving as good reasons on which to base a decision.

It is clear that individuals and societies have established widely varying rules of conduct over time, and thus must have had different understandings of the moral order. This statement of fact is accepted by all, but is interpreted differently by the deontologists and the teleologists. The teleologists would argue that these differences prove that there is no universal moral order, while the deontologists would argue that the moral order exists but is not yet fully understood (or as Hegel might say, it is still in the process of working out the knowledge of that which it is potentially). Thus, the gaps in understanding explain the differences among societies.

Regardless of whether there is agreement about the existence of universal rules, it can at least be argued that there are some moral rules of conduct which are present in all or nearly all societies, and which represent at least some of the beliefs held and practiced in our own society. Several examples of those universally accepted rules of conduct were presented earlier in the chapter.

While different societies, and the same society at different points in time, will interpret the meanings of those rules differently, there is considerable consistency in their acceptance as a part of the ideal moral order (at least in Western cultures). Truth telling, the sanctity of the individual, the sanctity of life, promise keeping, and the carrying out of obligations are fundamental to Western thought and thus are general rules which could serve to guide decision making by being "good reasons" for making a particular decision. Those good reasons, according to the deontologists, would serve as moral justification and defense of a decision after the fact, even if the outcomes of the decision were less than desirable (e.g., even if telling the truth means damaging the reputation of one's organizational superior). Two different deontological philosophies will be outlined here to illustrate this approach to ethics.

*Kant's Categorical Imperative.* According to Immanuel Kant's approach to deontology, the good decision is one which reason guides the actor to make, based upon respect for other rational beings. Kant suggests that the highest universal rule that should guide human action is the "Categorical Imperative," which has been formulated as "One ought only to act such that the principles of one's act could become a universal law of human action in a world in which one would hope to live" (Donaldson and Werhane, 1983:12). Applied to administrative ethics, the principles that guide the actions of the administrator ought to be principles which could be used to guide the actions of all members of society, resulting in a world in which the administrator would hope to live. There would be considerable agreement that truth telling, promise keeping, respect for the individual, and others mentioned above would be considered principles of this type, and should therefore help define the moral order on which administrative decisions will be based.

Some of the "universal rules" which have been suggested do serve as implicit rules guiding the behavior of administrators, and others' judgments about that behavior. For example, administrators are expected to tell the truth, to keep their promises, to carry out their obligations, and to respect the individual. These expectations grow out of a shared sense of a moral order, not out of laws or codes of ethics. When administrators (or any public officials) fail to abide by those standards, the failure might be dismissed as "typical," but would rarely be justified as ethical.

*Rawls' Theory of Justice.* A contemporary deontological theory which has gained much attention is that of John Rawls. Several scholars in the field have suggested that we rely heavily on Rawls' approach in developing an approach to administrative ethics, so it will be briefly outlined here. Rawls developed his theory by imagining an "original position" in which people behind a "veil of ignorance" would design a social order, including rights, duties, policies, and institutions, without having any knowledge of whether they as individuals would be among the best situated or the worst situated in that society (Rawls, 1971:11-12). Rawls argues that under such conditions a social order would be developed in which individuals and societies would judge their policies and institutions by the following principles:

*First Principle*

Each person is to have an equal right to the most extensive total system of equal basic liberty compatible with a similar system of liberty for all.

*Second Principle*

Social and economic inequalities are to be arranged so that they are both:
a) to the greatest benefit of the least advantaged . . .
b) attached to offices and positions open to all under conditions of fair equality of opportunity. (Rawls, 1971:302)

Thus, Rawls argues that "equal liberty" and principles of justice are two universal principles which all would agree are good, even in advance of any particular set of outcomes or consequences.

The deontological approach, generally and in the two specific forms outlined above, is not without its critics, among which are Frankena (1973), and MacIntyre (1984). The discoverability of the universal rules is undoubtedly the greatest challenge in this approach and certainly the area most open to criticism. Beyond that, the application of universal moral principles to everyday action is another area of difficulty which some say tends to promote moral rigidity, and as Dewey suggested, tends to lag behind social change and technological development. It is also pointed out that there are times when moral individuals would agree to make an exception to a universal rule, for example, by lying so as not to disclose to a person with murderous intentions the location of the intended victim. Critics of the deontological approach argue that because we would "suspend" the universal rule of truthtelling in this case, truthtelling must therefore not be a universal principle.

The criticisms of moral ridigity and the lack of absolute knowledge of the universal rules are sources of concern that should be addressed, but do not necessarily constitute an argument that such rules do not exist or that administrators should not make an effort to apply them in administrative practice. As argued earlier in this chapter, universal moral principles can be dynamic and open to change as they are interpreted in changing social conditions. In addition, there is considerable agreement that very similar basic moral principles are accepted in all or most societies, therefore the universal rules might be more "knowable" than it seems at first.

The criticism of the deontological approach regarding exceptions to those rules under certain circumstances suggests to some that the rules are therefore not universal, and the deontological perspective is false. To others it suggests that the moral theory must take into account the special nature of some situations, and that exceptions to universal moral principles can be permitted when a greater moral good is at stake (e.g., permitting lying in order to protect a life).

One example of taking into consideraton the special circumstances of a situation is Stuart Hampshire's discussion of public and private morality in which he suggests that the circumstances of official position must be accounted for, such as conflicts between one's obligation to the nation's security and one's obligations to tell the truth (Hampshire et al., 1978). These conflicts might only be resolved by giving priority to one over the other in a given instance. A public official has a special obligation to protect national security, thus justifying a lie if necessary. To deontologists, this need not suggest that universal moral principles do not exist.

### Teleology: Consequentialism

Many philosophers and writers on the subject of administrative ethics take a teleological approach which focuses on the consequences of decisions and then judges the rightness or wrongness of the decision exclusively by the outcomes it produces. In this view, there are no moral principles which can provide *a priori* justifications for a decision without first assessing the desirability of the outcomes of the decision. For example, from a teleological perspective, telling the truth cannot be judged *a priori* as a good or right thing to do. If telling the truth leads to outcomes that are considered good, then telling the truth is a good thing to do. If telling the truth leads to outcomes that are not considered good, then telling the truth is wrong.

In terms of understanding the moral order, a teleological approach is relativistic in that no moral principles are considered lasting or absolute since the principles that guide actions will always be judged in terms of the values associated with the outcomes. The most commonly known forms of teleology—egoism, act utilitarianism, and rule utilitarianism—will be explored in the next section.

*Egoism.* This form of teleological theory can be characterized as a "view that everyone ought to promote his own self-interest" or that "one acts in a morally acceptable way if and only if one acts in such a way as to secure the greatest possible benefit for oneself" (Feldman, 1978:80). This theory is one of pure self-interest, maximizing the long-term pleasure of the individual. The theory assumes no altruistic or community oriented motives on the part of individuals, though such motives might guide the behaviors of *some* individuals because it brings them great personal pleasure.

In terms of administrative ethics, egoism would suggest that public administrators act morally when they pursue their own long-term self-interest, not when they focus on the public interest for its own sake.

The theory of egoism clearly focuses on consequences of actions (the amount of pleasure or "utility" the act provides for the individual), and holds no universal principles as guiding forces. The theory has few advocates among moral philosophers, and many refute it entirely. One telling refutation rests on the argument that if the manager of a pension fund could successfully steal the pension money and get away with it, then it would in fact be immoral *not* to steal the money, since maximization of personal pleasure would clearly be gained by stealing the money, not by acting on behalf of the pensioners (Feldman, 1978:95-96). Since this is not generally acceptable, egoism must be refuted.

Though egoism is difficult to support, many people would argue that it is the very basis of capitalism, and thus a crucial element of the society in which public administrators in the

United States and other capitalist countries must act. In addition, many people behave in such a way as to reflect egoism. Should it, then, be seriously considered as the basis of administrative ethics? The best response to this is probably provided not by some moral philosopher, but by Adam Smith, a most eloquent defender of capitalism but who also provides a strong criticism of self-interested behavior as a basis for social action. Though Adam Smith believed that people often act in a purely self-interested fashion and that an economic system based on assumptions of individuality would be best, he did not believe that people *ought to* act in such a way in all matters. In fact, in *The Theory of Moral Sentiments*, he argued that personal virtue and ethical behavior must be the cornerstone of an economic system (Smith, 1982). Since ethics and the moral order are based on what we believe "ought to" be rather than what "is," Adam Smith's defense of capitalism should not be interpreted as a defense of egoism—probably just the opposite is true.

Two other forms of teleological theories have considerably more to support them: act utilitarianism and rule utilitarianism. Utilitarianism judges moral worth according to the amount of good achieved by a course of action. Thus, there is a need to anticipate and measure the amount of "good" or "utility" which accrues to individuals and balance that against the expected "pain," in order to determine which course of action to take.

*Mill's Act Utilitarianism.* John Stuart Mill's act utilitarian argument goes as follows:

actions are right in proportion as they tend to promote happiness, wrong as they tend to produce the reverse of happiness. By "happiness" is intended pleasure, and the absence of pain. (Mill, 1957:10)

Act utilitarianism judges the morality of each individual action based on the cumulative consequences of the action—the amount and balance of pleasure or pain which accrues to all of the individuals involved. The course of action which would promote the greatest aggregate pleasure would be judged the moral course of action. This approach to understanding and applying the "moral order" to administrative decisions would lead the administrator to ask "If I do 'X' how much good will accrue among the affected people?" This focus leads the administrator to make a decision which will result in satisfaction for the greatest number and in that way determine what is right and good (therefore moral) in that situation. The administrator does not follow any moral principle which, in advance of the calculations of aggregate utility, would indicate what course of action would be most moral in a particular case. The administrator also avoids generalizing beyond individual cases; each act is judged according to its own merits and consequences.

*Brandt's Rule Utilitarianism.* Rule utilitarianism accepts the notion that certain moral principles can be derived from experience and can form a type of moral code to be followed by members of a society. However, the moral principles are not universal (for they are appropriate for a single society at a given point in time), and they are not "good" intrinsically, but rather are judged "good" because following such rules would result in the greatest overall aggregate utility. Thus, rule utilitarianism differs from act utilitarianism in that some generalizable rules of conduct can be established. But these rules of conduct are different from the deontological approach in the ways specified above. Richard Brandt's theory of rule utilitarianism can be stated as follows:

An act is right if and only if it would not be prohibited by the moral code ideal for the society. (Brandt, 1971:331)

The "moral code" is not universal, eternal, or intrinsically good. A moral code, according to Brandt, is ideal for a society if, in practice, it would produce at least as much "good per person" as any other moral code (Brandt, 1971:331).

Applied to public administration ethics, rule utilitarianism would be something like a deontological approach in that there would be an agreed-upon moral code, but that code would be subject to ongoing calculations of aggregate utilities rather than accepted as lasting or universal. An ideal moral code might be identified which results in the greatest "good per person," but as circumstances change, the calculus of "good per person" might require a change in the moral code.

One criticism of utilitarianism is based mainly on intuition or common sense:

It has seemed to many philosophers, and it appears to be supported by the convictions of common sense, that we distinguish as a matter of principle between the claims of liberty and right on the one hand and the desirability of increasing aggregate social welfare on the other; and that we give a certain priority, if not absolute weight, to the former. (Rawls, 1971:27-28)

The utilitarian approach to determining the morality of an act is often criticized on the basis that it allows possible injustices to an individual or a minority when the outcomes of those injustices result in greater overall "good" for the majority. For example, the enslavement of a small number of people in order to work as servants for the larger group might be considered morally justifiable according to the utilitarian theory because it results in the greatest amount of utility, or the greatest amount of good (in this case satisfaction) for the majority. Act utilitarianism is clearly more susceptible to this line of criticism than is rule utilitarianism. Rule utilitarianism could well support a moral code which prohibits such enslavement because such a rule, if applied broadly, in the long run might lead to less "good per person" than would a rule which supports equal liberty, for example.

Another response to the criticism that utilitarianism potentially allows injustices is that the definition of "utility" need not be limited to the notions of pleasure and pain. Some utilitarians define the relevant utilities very broadly, including liberty, equality, and justice as desirable outcomes. Thus, the measurement of the aggregate utility resulting from an act might be quite different than if only "satisfaction" were considered. It must be remembered, though, that liberty, equality, and justice, even if included in the calculation, are not considered good in and of themselves, but deemed desirable outcomes because they are viewed as contributing to overall utility or satisfaction. Thus, the same concepts are viewed very differently from the teleological and deontological perspectives.

## Deontology, Teleology, and Administrative Action

Deontology and teleology are the two broad ways of thinking about the moral order. Both can contribute to our understanding of a moral order, and both are open to significant criticism. But, how does this apply to public administration and to administrative ethics?

According to the framework developed in the previous chapter, in order to be considered ethical, an administrator must abide by the moral order in making decisions. Therefore, the administrator must have some knowledge of what the moral order is, and how it can be used in making decisions. If the moral order is made up of some universal principles that all administrators are expected to know and follow, then that has one set of implications for administrative ethics. If, on the other hand, the moral order is that which can be judged only by the aggregate utilities associated with the outcomes of a decision, then the administrator needs to use a different set of skills and measures in determining what is "right."

Since philosophers have been unable to come to an agreement about how to think about morality and the "good," it is unlikely that the ambiguity associated with these two ways of thinking will be resolved in a framework for understanding administrative ethics. Although this author finds a deontological approach more defensible, there is no widespread agreement about the existence of universally applicable moral rules. Such lack of agreement is ably conveyed by Ralph Clark Chandler in his discussion of the development of a code of ethics for the American Society for Public Administration (Chandler, 1983b). This might very well necessitate developing an approach to administrative ethics which is tenable under either deontological or teleological assumptions. One way to determine if such an approach is possible is by examining one of the guides which has been suggested for administrative ethics—an emphasis on the democratic ethos—in terms of its deontological and teleological interpretations.

Because of the problems of overreliance on scientific analysis, empiricism, and other ostensibly "value-free" tools, there has been a resurgence of interest in the "democratic ethos" of public administration as the appropriate ethical guide for public administrators. Mark Lilla (1981) argues that the democratic ethos was widely shared among members of the field of public administration through the 1940's, and as evidence cites the Friedrich/Finer debates. These scholarly debates about the role of public administrators revolved around the notions of professional expertise, the public interest, and relationships to elected officials, all of which, Lilla says, reflected the sincere effort to understand the Constitution and legal history in order to interpret what the administrative role should be. Lilla suggests that both sides in the debates rested on the democratic ethos, and Lilla sees this as far superior to the more recent reliance on scientific analysis which strays from the democratic ethos. As Lilla argues, too much emphasis on scientific analysis results in training policy analysts who are unprepared to answer any questions about the morality of what they do, or the relationship between their work and the democratic process (Lilla, 1981).

This raises an immediate and important question: What is the relationship between the concept of a "democratic ethos" and the moral order? Is the democratic ethos *synonymous* with the moral order? Or does the democratic ethos provide a process for *discovering* an appropriate moral order? Or, finally, can any moral judgments about a democratic ethos be made at all— could it be that a democratic ethos is *morally neutral*? Each of these viewpoints has been suggested and will be explored in what follows.

Emmette Redford has described three ideals or values on which democratic morality is based:

The basic ideal is that persons are the units of value in social arrangements. . . . This is the individualistic foundation of democratic morality. . . . The second ideal is that all men have worth deserving social recognition. . . . This is the egalitarian component of democratic morality. The third ideal is that personal worth is most fully protected and enlarged by the action of those whose worth is assumed . . . liberty exists only through *participation either in decision making or in control of leaders who make the decisions.* (Redford, 1969:6)

He suggested, then, that the Constitution was intended to outline the process whereby the democratic values would be carried out. This would appear to assume that a democratic ethos rests upon, and is synonymous with, an agreed-upon moral order. Thus the democratic ethos represents the ideal moral code and members of society are obligated to support the moral precepts. This can either be viewed as a deontological argument, or at a minimum a rule utilitarian argument if the "universe" to which the values are applied is limited to a single society.

Another interpretation of the democratic ethos in administrative practice is one presented by Michael Harmon:

In accepting the existentialists' contention that ultimate and transcendental values do not exist, we are forced to confront the knotty problem of patterning administrative and political systems to accommodate this notion. . . . Individual needs and values are presumed to be legitimate in part because of the lack of evidence to the contrary. . . . The existentialist perspective suggests that the public administrator must attempt, however inadequately, to understand the relationship of his own values and motives to questions of public policy, and to create a climate in which those to whom he is legally responsible are encouraged to do likewise and to assert their values in the political arena. (Harmon, 1971:180-182)

Harmon then describes Thorson's position, which argues that because there is no ultimate moral order, government is required to keep the way open for involvement and change. In this way Thorson provides a justification for a democratic form of government. By rejecting the notion that the moral order can be known, Harmon and Thorson make the more utilitarian argument that the utilities associated with democracy are greater than the utilities associated with other forms of government. Therefore, the ethical administrator should be more democratic.

In relating these arguments to the Constitution, Redford sees the Constitution as resting on the already agreed-upon moral order. The Constitution is not in itself the "end" but rather reflects the true moral order which includes the ideals of individual value, equality, and participation. Harmon and Thorson might view the Constitution as providing the process for discovering the moral principles of a society. Since the moral principles cannot be otherwise known, or independently justified, it is important to hold the democratic process as somewhat "sacred" in an instrumental sense—whatever results from the democratic process can only be judged by whether the appropriate process was used in arriving at the outcome. Clearly these two views of the democratic ethos provide very different cues to the administrator trying to act in an ethical manner.

So, much along the lines of the ongoing struggle to define the public interest, we now have difficulties defining what a democratic ethos means in terms of the ethical practice of public administration. Different approaches to moral reasoning and justifications will lead us to take different approaches to interpreting and applying Constitutional principles and other democratic norms.

Let us now look at a third interpretation of the role of the Constitution. John Rohr in *Ethics for Bureaucrats* (1978) argues that the Constitution and Supreme Court opinions interpreting that Constitution should be the cornerstone of bureaucratic ethics. The moral basis for this argument is that administrators must abide by their promises—in this case their oath to uphold the Constitution taken at the time of their initial employment. Rohr does not argue that the Constitution represents a superior moral order (though he doesn't necessarily argue against this idea either). Instead he argues that it represents "regime values," is therefore legitimate, and that the moral imperative for administrators is the keeping of one's oaths or promises. He continues this line of reasoning in *To Run A Constitution* (1986b) in which he argues that it is the obligation of public administrators to uphold the Constitution and its separation of powers—not because the Constitution and the separation of powers are intrinsically good, but because they represent regime values which the administrator has promised to uphold. In this sense, promise keeping may be viewed as a universal rule, but nothing about the Constitution itself would be viewed as inherently obligatory in the absence of such an oath. The Constitution and the democratic ethos might be thought of as morally neutral, even though the public administrator does have a moral obligation to uphold it because of the promise made to do so, and because these *are* the regime values.

Lilla would probably view the existence of all three arguments in a very positive way—debate about the notion of the democratic ethos, even without a resolution, is an indication that the democratic ethos is taken seriously. All three interpretations place value on the Constitution, its structures and its principles, and go a long way toward guiding administrative ethics.

However, the differences among the interpretations are not unimportant. For example, if the moral order reflected by the Constitution is, in fact, universal, then the ethical judgments that are based on that moral order would apply not just to our own policies and actions, but to those of other nations as well. Since we do make moral judgments about the practices of other nations based upon value principles contained in our Constitution (e.g., judgments about the immorality of human rights violations), this is an indication that the Constitution represents something more than just a statement guiding the governance of our own nation. It might be argued that aspects of the Constitution reflect universal moral principles which ought to guide all action. This deontological interpretation of the Constitution and the moral order would argue for rejecting a teleological approach to administrative ethics that views a moral order as uncertain or relative.

## Conclusion

The differences in perspectives discussed in this section illuminate not only the difficulties in defining a democratic ethos, or the relationship between the Constitution and the moral order, but also the difficult issues that are a part of the history, and thus the current context of public administration ethics. Clearly this discussion has not resolved the complexities of understanding our moral order, nor the complexities associated with making administrative decisions in a democratic society. But it may have served to illustrate the point that in developing an approach to administrative ethics, how one thinks about the moral order might determine what one recommends in the way of administrative action and what outcomes can be anticipated.

Related to the framework of administrative ethics developed in the previous chapter, this discussion indicates that references to the "moral order" are going to be open to disagreements in interpretation. Can the framework for ethical administration be useful without resolving these disagreements? The answer would seem to be "yes," for reasons which follow.

In practice, administrators are expected to hold to the types of principles usually described as universal rules (e.g., truth telling, promise keeping, the sanctity of life). It usually won't matter whether one argues that these represent a fundamental moral order or whether they represent valued outcomes by which utilitarians would measure aggregate utility in judging the morality of an act. If administrators are, in practice, expected to adhere to those moral principles, then there is reason to include those in an approach to administrative ethics. This doesn't resolve the philosophical questions, but it does emphasize that in practice sufficient agreement about principles exists so that development of an approach to administrative ethics can progress.

There is also general agreement that the rights, restrictions, and other general guidelines in the Constitution are important considerations for the administrator. It usually won't matter whether those are important considerations because the Constitution is a reflection of our fundamental moral order, or because the Constitution is a means for assuring maximum participation in the development of a moral order. The actions of the administrator will usually be the same, and therefore the Constitution should be an important consideration in an approach or theory of administrative ethics. The debate over how and why the Constitution is important might be left to the scholars, while practitioners would be able to continue upholding and supporting Constitutional principles without the full justification and rationale for doing so already in place.

There will be times, however, when the way one thinks about the moral order will influence the decision to be made. For example, when the rights, duties, and obligations outlined in the Constitution come into conflict with other moral considerations (e.g., when the moral conviction of the sanctity of human life comes into conflict with legitimate laws and court decisions upholding the death penalty in a particular case, or when constitutionally-defined institutions are shown *not* to promote the egalitarian values that democracy is presumed to be built upon), then the primacy given to the Constitution in the moral order might influence the resolution of the dilemma. For that reason, it is important to understand the different ways of thinking about ethics and the moral order, and it is important to continue the dialogue about our understanding of the nature of the moral order. But it should not stand in the way of developing an approach to administrative ethics that draws upon the many areas of existing agreement.

Examining our understanding of the fundamental moral order has provided many clues and contributions to the understanding of what it means to be an ethical administrator. Administrative ethics is still very much in the process of working out "that which it is potentially," but there is sufficient information about our understanding of the moral order that can serve as a guide for developing an approach to administrative ethics. The approach, though, is quite dependent on some resolution of the closely related issue of the *role* of public administrators. What role are public administrators expected to play in the development and application of morality in public life? If administrators are expected by the society to carry out only what others have defined as the "right" thing to do, then that is a very different role from being expected by the society to aid in developing and defining our sense of the moral order. Societal expectations of the public administrator have changed over the past decades, and will be explored in the next section.

## THE ROLE OF THE PUBLIC ADMINISTRATOR

Waldo (1980) argued that it was only about a century ago that administration became a self-conscious enterprise, and thus is a relatively new discipline of study (though certainly not new in practice). In becoming a self-conscious enterprise, public administration had to make the transition from an unreflected-upon endeavor to what is now often called a profession. The need to develop a theory of administration much less a theory of administrative ethics did not exist or was not recognized until public administration became a self-conscious enterprise.

In the course of this century three important changes in the role of the public administrator have been the subject of considerable reflection and influence, and are highlighted below.

First of all, it has been recognized that over time the administrator has become more than one who administers the policies of others; the administrator has become a policymaker in many ways. This has forced changes in both theory (away from the politics/administration dichotomy) and in practice (away from unthinking development of precedent-setting rules and procedures). This illustrates the need for a theory of administrative ethics, and focuses attention on the policy-making aspects of the administrative role.

Second, as government grew and legislators became more removed from their constituents and unable to fully develop public policies, the public began to demand more responsiveness as well as responsibility from public administrators in the bureaucracy. Thus the administrator was urged to become advocate, change agent, and responsive politician as well as administrator of policies. This changing role of the administrator requires a different approach to decision making than would policy implementation without expectations of responsiveness and the attendant political implications. In the more broadly defined role, value implications of policy decisions and responsive actions must be considered a vital part of the decision process. Thus, administrative decision making becomes increasingly important to the ethical outcomes of policies. In addition, such an expanded role exposes the administrator to many more ethical dilemmas.

Third, as the role of the administrator expanded into the policy-making and advocacy realm, the expertise of the administrators increased and the role of "professional" developed. Being a "professional" implies a specific area of expertise, and also implies a value construct which would guide the actions of members of the profession. It isn't clear that public administration has fully developed such a value construct, but if and when this value construct conflicts with the other moral standards imposed upon the administrator, there is an ethical problem of significant importance. Professional ethics and public ethics are sometimes at odds with one another and this is an important dimension of the external environment of public administration. As public administrators found it necessary to take on policy-making responsibilities, and society began demanding responsiveness from administrators, and the "profession" of public administration began to develop, new ethical considerations arose with significant importance for the development of a framework for administrative ethics.

Each of these major changes in the role of the public administrator will be discussed below.

### The Administrator as Policymaker

Mark Lilla (1981) argued that the movement away from the democratic ethos as the primary guide for administrative behavior began with the advent of scientific approaches to decision-making in the 1960's and with values clarification approaches to ethics, which failed to convey the intrinsic importance of democratic values.

A different argument is that the shift in focus away from democratic values can be attributed to our failure to acknowledge that administrators were in fact making public policy and therefore had a fundamental role in, and responsibility for, upholding the Constitution and the democratic ethos. When the administrator is viewed as important to the policy process, different obligations are implied than would be true if the administrator is seen only as a policy implementor.

This failure to acknowledge and consider the changing role of the public administrator had wide-ranging consequences in terms of administrative ethics. The shift back toward the political nature of administration which had existed prior to this century's civil service reforms occurred in practice and was virtually ignored in theory. Theory continued to be guided by the outdated notion of a politics/administration dichotomy. This meant that administrators found it necessary to play a policy making (political) role, but to do so without the guidance of a theory which legitimated and gave ethical guidance to that role.

The role of policymaker requires that administrators make value judgments about the policies they are involved in making. But, the theory that has guided administrative actions since the civil service reforms was one of neutral competence, which left the false impression that administrative judgments were purely objective and therefore not subject to ethical inquiry. Case 2.A illustrates this point.

*Case 2.A*

Following the Watergate scandal and other revelations of Nixon era abuses of intelligence gathering, federal intelligence agencies were required to change many of their rules and standard practices. The use of listening devices and various other practices were restricted. Reflecting on the changes, one intelligence operative commented that there really were no ethical questions of concern to the agency personnel either before or after the changes. From the perspective of the agency, this was simply a question of rule changes. Intelligence agency personnel need not make judgments about the ethics of wire taps and bugging devices, they need only follow whatever rules are provided for them by their superiors and elected officials at the time of the activity.

Clearly administrators *are* expected to make judgments about the ethics of their actions, and there needs to be a theory that guides such judgments. Several alternatives have been proposed. The New Public Administration called for more democratic (Harmon, 1971) and more equitable (Hart, 1974) administrative behavior as a way of guiding administrative ethics. Waldo (1980) states that it is the role of the administrator to represent the collectivity, and Chandler (1983a) suggests that the administrator should take seriously the dual roles of administrator and citizen in developing the moral order or seeking ends which are in the public interest. Chandler advocates a "trusteeship" role for public administrators in terms of developing policies which are in the public interest. But an approach has yet to be developed that fully legitimates the policymaking role of the public administrator and which provides adequate guidance as to the moral foundations of administrative ethics. This aspect of the administrator's environment will provide continuing challenges in the development of the theory and practice of administrative ethics.

## Public Demand for Administrative Responsiveness

The political role of policy-making was not the only new role in which administrators often found themselves. The public began to perceive that they had more access to administrators than they did to their legislators, and so began to expect responsiveness from administrators. But being responsive to client needs can raise difficult practical as well as ethical questions because the responsive decision might set a precedent for similar decisions in the future.

Rosen (1982) states that the *responsible* administrator must consider the precedents set by their decisions. Clearly, decisions do not occur in isolation of one another, and therefore the administrator must be both responsive, and responsible for the precedents set. The political nature of the job requires that the administrator be responsive but the administrative nature of the job requires a concern for consistency, order, and responsibility. As John Locke wrote, "freedom of men under government is . . . not to be subject to the inconstant, uncertain, unknown, arbitrary will of another man" (Locke, 1952:15).

An example of the tension between responsiveness and responsibility appears in Case 2.B.

*Case 2.B*

A social service administrator must make a decision about how to categorize property owned by elderly welfare applicants in order to determine eligibility. The elderly applicant might own a modest home but have no other assets or means of support. The administrator might find it difficult to require that the person sell the home and deplete that reserve before applying for welfare once again, this time in even more desperate straits. Younger welfare applicants might be expected to give up their homes, but their prospects for successfully making the adjustment and at some point recovering financially are considerably greater than the prospects for the elderly applicant. Applying different standards to the young and the old has some appeal because it allows responsiveness to the differing needs of clients. On the other hand, is it *just* to apply different standards to the elderly than one does to the younger applicants, and what kind of precedent would this set?

In making a decision about this case the administrator is expected to be responsive to the needs of the elderly, but also to make responsible decisions. In determining what is responsible, the administrator might examine the consequences of the elderly being forced to give up their homes versus the consequences of the same requirement for younger applicants (a teleological or utilitarian approach to making the decision). Or, the administrator might pose the question in terms of whether some universal moral principle requires that all applicants be treated equally in order to be fair to all (a more deontological approach). Different approaches to the question might result in different and conflicting answers for the administrator. This illustrates the dilemmas of balancing the responsiveness role with other aspects of the administrative role. How one defines the morality and responsibility, as well as disagreements about whether such discretionary judgments should be made by administrators at all, will influence the resolution of the dilemmas and should be accommodated in any approach to administrative ethics.

The framework of administrative ethics developed in the first chapter rests firmly and significantly on a particular view of the administrative role—one of the individually responsible, policy-making administrator who is also an organizational member. Administrators who do not consciously perceive themselves to be policymakers (or part of the political realm) will find it is either not necessary or not legitimate for them to critique, question, or even understand the goals of society and the moral implications of the policies they are implementing. They can focus on the implementation of a law without thought to its value implications because they perceive their role as one focused on structures, rules, and good implementation rather than values, moral orders, and policy outcomes. Such a view falls outside the definition of ethical administrative action developed earlier. Although some administrators still hold this view about their role, it is one that fails to acknowledge the reality of their work and their role. In other words, this is a false perception, though one not uncommon among public administrators.

When the administrator is perceived as playing a governance or change agent role (as Harmon and others have argued public administrators are obliged to play) then the role that values, critique, independence, and moral judgments play changes dramatically. This view of the administrator is becoming the standard perception, though it is not always received with strong support (Davis, 1969). But, if the public administrator does participate in the governance function, then it is very important that administrators know how to think about the moral order of society, have some moral foundation on which to make decisions, and be able to carry those decisions out within the complex set of obligations outlined earlier.

## The "Profession" of Public Administration

Along with changing social expectations of public administrators came a new self-perception among those in the field. There was a growing perception that the expertise and training necessary to practice many areas of public administration justified viewing those administrators as "professionals" in their own right.

That emerging professional role carried with it the inclination, or perhaps obligation, to play the role of advocate for certain client groups, and to demand more discretionary authority to make policy decisions in individual cases. The sense of professionalism increased the independence of the professional (and arguably improved effectiveness as well) and became an important factor in explaining the overall increase in administrative discretion.

With increased professionalism, the likelihood that the administrator will encounter competing value structures also increased—professional norms and values might begin to compete with democratic, organizational, or personal norms and values. Debra Stewart (1985b) provides an excellent example of how such conflict might occur, and how it would affect administrative ethics. Medical professionals at a community mental hospital turned away a severely mentally disturbed child. The medical professionals were attempting to meet their professional obligations by treating the patients already in the hospital "and felt that to add a severely disturbed child to this environment would diminish their ability to cure the less disturbed patients" (Stewart, 1985b:20). Shortly after being turned away, the child committed suicide and the decision to turn away the child came under considerable criticism from the community. Thus, Stewart suggests, "while this response might be professionally appropriate, it was . . . cruel and irresponsible" from the point of view of others (Stewart, 1985b:20-21). The professional value structure seems, in this case, to be at odds with community values.

It is often hard to judge whether professional ethics are adequately representative of the moral order, and thus whether they are a good means of informing administrative decisions. As argued by Bok (1978) and Goldman (1980), professions all too often set themselves artificially apart from the moral order and society, defending this separation on this basis of paternalism, expertise, and secrecy. In the case of public administration this separation of the professional role from the general moral order is exhibited in the distinction made between public and private morality which is often used to justify immoral actions by public officials. The justification is based upon the alleged conflict between a moral principle and other obligations attached to the public office which require a different approach to morality. However, Bok and Goldman both argue that the public nature of a position would excuse officials from the rules of private morality on very few occasions, considerably less often than the justification is currently used.

Sissela Bok, in her book *Lying*, states that "when political representatives or entire governments arrogate to themselves the right to lie, they take power from the public that would not have been given up voluntarily" (Bok, 1978:185). She asks, "Do we want to live in a society where public officials can resort to deceit and manipulation whenever they decide that an exceptional crisis has arisen?" and then draws the conclusion that "only those deceptive practices which can be openly debated and consented to in advance are justifiable in a democracy" (Bok, 1978:190-191).

Alan Goldman in *The Moral Foundations of Professional Ethics* finds that:

When we recognize that the same moral framework applies to both the private and public domains, that within it rights are prior to utilities but ordered in relation to each other, and that the politician more often than the rest of us must make decisions with a context of conflicting rights, the paradox dissolves. The moral framework for political decision does not differ from the usual, but the occasions for its application in the political context do. People indeed must occasionally be lied to, deceived or coerced by political acts, but only when more fundamental rights are at stake. (Goldman, 1980:71)

For Goldman the politician is the policymaker so the statement above would also apply to the policy-making aspect of the administrative role. The rights Goldman refers to are such rights as life, individual autonomy and equality, freedom from unwarranted interference, self respect, and security in expectation. He argues from a deontological perspective that those rights serve as universal rules of moral conduct which are prior to any consideration of the general utility or satisfaction associated with the application of the right in a particular instance.

The main point within the professionalism context is that in almost all cases the public administrator as professional has the same obligations to uphold the moral order as does a private citizen or nonprofessional. In effect, this places primacy to upholding the moral order over the rights, privileges, or responsibilities of one's professional position. This confers an obligation upon the public administrator to consider the moral order in making all policy decisions, and not rely strictly upon the generally accepted practices of the profession or be limited to the moral principles that have been institutionalized in law.

Bok and Goldman suggest that the professions should be expected to abide by common moral standards rather than separate standards in the vast majority of cases. Therefore, professionalism may be a source of technical expertise, but the ethical code of the profession should for the most part adhere to the common social code practiced (or at least espoused) by private individuals. Both arrived at this conclusion by focusing mainly on a deontological assumption that there are identifiable moral codes in society (which would preclude lying) and that the moral code should have precedence over most other obligations of the administrator (e.g., the obligation to the position or organization).

How is an administrator to deal with the competing thought systems regarding the moral order, with the sometimes competing moral standards to be applied, and with the ambiguities associated with the administrative role in the moral order? Various philosophical approaches have been used in attempting to deal with, or perhaps resolve, those inconsistencies and ambiguities. Two of those philosophical traditions will be addressed in the concluding section of this chapter in order to enhance the general understanding of administrative ethics, contribute to the clarification of ambiguities present in the social context, and increase knowledge of how these traditions have influenced the history of public administration.

## PHILOSOPHICAL MATRICES FOR RESOLVING AMBIGUITY IN ADMINISTRATIVE ETHICS

How can public administrators, individually and as a group, work out the occasional moral conflicts that will rise out of the competing demands and expectations placed on the administrator by society, clients, elected officials and others? Also, what tools are available to public administrators to help them critique the guidance they are given, and provide a basis for questioning the various viewpoints that they and others hold? The traditions of moral philosophy and political philosophy can contribute a great deal to these efforts.

As pointed out in Chapter 1, one of the great weaknesses in the development of administrative ethics is the lack of consultation with our philosophical traditions. Moral philosophy (ethics) and political philosophy both contain many approaches to resolving the critical dilemmas facing administrators today. Both have contributed much to defining the role and context within which public administration is practiced, and utilizing them in resolving the resulting dilemmas makes good sense.

## Moral Philosophy

The previously presented outline of the deontological and teleological approaches to thinking about the moral order is perhaps the clearest demonstration of the relevance of moral philosophy to public administration ethics. However, this philosophical tradition has much more to offer. First, knowledge of moral philosophy helps train individuals in the logic and careful reasoning necessary to present cogent and defensible justifications for a point of view, or a decision. It not only helps in understanding how to present an argument, but also in identifying morally significant issues. All of those skills are necessary for successfully engaging in ethical deliberation and dialogue.

Second, moral philosophy provides a source of critique and questioning, as Leys (1944) pointed out. It suggests opposing arguments and points of view that will help to enhance an administrator's understanding of a situation or ethical dilemma, and his or her ability to defend a decision. However, it is important to heed Mark Lilla's (1981) warning that simply training public administrators in ethics, without any grounding in the democratic ethos, could well result in their ability to carefully argue a point of view without really being able to make a judgment about whether that view is morally right or wrong. So many opposing viewpoints are present in moral philosophy, that an improperly trained individual might simply view moral philosophy as a shopping list of defenses for any course of action the individual happens to prefer.

Third, the study and application of moral philosophy provides an opportunity for the administrator to gain expertise in an approach to decision making which does not focus on the individual, necessarily, but that suggests ways of considering the impact of the decision on the collective, of considering fraternity as well as individuality. In other words, a broad exposure to moral philosophy provides alternatives to ethical egoism.

Perhaps most importantly, moral philosophy can *complement* scientific analysis which is widely purported to be neutral, providing answers or decisions based on *facts* without making overt value judgments. But science alone has been shown to be too narrow and confining. "The history of intellectual life during the past two hundred years has imposed ever more severe restrictions on what counts as genuine knowledge and on limits of rational argument . . . strictly speaking, we cannot even meaningfully talk about values, for values lie outside the world of facts and meaningful propositions about these facts" (Bernstein, 1976:xxiii).

Bernstein describes the virtues of the traditions of a philosophy of science and empiricism as the insistence upon clarity and rigor and a "healthy skepticism toward unbridled speculation," but that those traditions "have turned into suffocating strait jackets" as values were excluded from consideration (Bernstein, 1976:xxii-xxiii).

Although the traditional concept of the philosophy of science cannot serve as a guide in ethical decision making because it does not include overt consideration of value issues, it may still be able to contribute to a framework for public administration ethics because it provides guidance in identifying problems, gathering information, and thinking logically about problems. Those are valuable skills in ethical as well as rational decision making. If this type of skill is tempered or complemented by increasing recognition that values influence what the scientist chooses to observe or to study, and values are an influence on the data gathered and its interpretation, then value choices can take on an appropriate role in administrative action. Moral philosophy and scientific analysis, together, can provide a healthy combination of rigor and ethical considerations.

### Political Philosophy

Political Philosophy is regaining popularity as a source of guidance for resolving problems associated with administrative ethics. The discussions of the democratic ethos presented earlier are an example of this, as are some of the more recent works dealing with the role of the administrator. For example, Chandler (1983a) examines the role of the administrator by comparing the Roman and Athenian interpretations of the administrative role *vis a vis* the role of the citizen.

Another dimension of political philosophy that is referred to is political writing such as the Federalist papers, which contain some interpretations of the moral principles contained within the Constitution. Madison argued in favor of the ratification of the Constitution because it would create a government that would overcome criticisms that "measures are too often decided, not according to the rules of justice and the rights of the minor party, but by the superior force of an interested and overbearing majority" (Commager, 1949:9). In other words, the Constitution was thought to provide reasons for making just decisions that would override the interests and preferences of the majority when the rights of the individual were involved. Presumably this would mean that aggregate utility would not be maximized in every case, thus making Madison's argument appear to be a deontological one as opposed to a utilitarian one.

The recent emphasis on constitutionalism, the democratization of the workplace, responsiveness, and participativeness draw upon political philosophy as providing the justification for those objectives and actions. These address issues associated with the administrative role as well as the standards which the administrator is expected to apply. Political philosophy can, and will, be helpful in exploring those issues and thus in developing a framework for administrative ethics.

Political philosophy provides various interpretations of the relationship between the state and the moral order (e.g., Hobbes, Mill) and the expectations for good government and good citizenship (e.g., Aristotle, Plato). Machiavelli's writings are an excellent example of the argument for separating private morality from public positions (Hampshire et al., 1978:49). The list of such contributions is seemingly endless. Increasingly, the value of these sources is being recognized as evidenced by exchanges such as that found in a 1984 special issue of the *Public Administration Review* in which "Citizenship and Public Administration" was the topic, and many of the articles refer to the writings of the Greco-Roman period, Hobbes, Walter Lippmann,

Aristotle, Adam Smith, as well as the writings of our own Founders (Frederickson and Chandler, 1984). Clearly political philosophy can help in understanding the social and historical context of public administration, and provides much insight into ethical approaches to administration.

## Conclusion

The philosophical traditions are central to understanding the changing context of public administration. These traditions highlight areas of conflict and contrast of viewpoints, but also point to the many areas on which there is considerable agreement. The philosophical traditions provide some of the necessary tools for recognizing and resolving the ethical dilemmas of administration.

What, then, does this mean for the theoretical framework for administrative ethics which was developed in Chapter 1? This chapter has demonstrated that there is a moral order which can be understood and followed by administrators in making ethical decisions. Although there is not total agreement on the nature, source, or content of that moral order, there is *sufficient* agreement to provide the necessary basis for public administration ethics.

Also demonstrated in this chapter is that society has many expectations of public administrators and the role of the administrator is broad, though not all-encompassing. This helps to support the idea that administrators have an active, though not unconstrained, role in interpreting and implementing the moral order in the course of their work. There are many sources of guidance in determining the nature of the expectations of the administrator, and in making moral judgments in administrative decisions. Political philosophy and moral philosophy are both helpful in identifying methods, procedures and structures associated with good government and good administration (i.e., process issues). In terms of the content dimension of administrative ethics, political philosophy provides a wealth of guidance in terms of the values, rights, and duties associated with "the good life" and the good society. Moral philosophy offers an added dimension in that it provides input into thinking about and deciding upon certain moral convictions and then applying those to action. Political philosophy provides many ideas, but moral philosophy can contribute to the critique of those ideas and to their application to administrative practice.

Thus, the theoretical framework has been shown to be consistent with, and workable within, the social and historical context of public administration. In the next chapter, the more immediate environment of the public organization will be explored in terms of how the theoretical framework fits within that context, and how organizations will influence the ethics of public administration.

# 3

# THE ORGANIZATIONAL CONTEXT OF PUBLIC ADMINISTRATION

The social and historical context of public administration, important because it helps administrators interpret their roles and obligations in society, is rivaled by another equally important set of influences on administrators' actions—the organizational context within which they carry out their work. Exploring the organizational context will be beneficial in explaining how obligations to public organizations are perceived by administrators, how organizations influence the role definition of public administrators, and how organizational structures and values influence the decision making of administrators.

The organizational context is a critical element to consider in a theoretical framework of administrative ethics, because the organization imposes (and administrators accept) a new set of obligations, pressures and constraints. The organization will in some ways determine who engages in ethical deliberation, what is considered ethical, as well as the range of options available to administrators who are attempting to make the "ethical" decision. Therefore, we must determine whether it is possible for administrators to act according to the expectations laid out in the administrative ethics framework developed in Chapter 1, given these organizational constraints.

The organizational context of public administration will be explored in terms of the following characteristics: (1) expectations of organizational loyalty which sometimes conflict with other loyalties and obligations; (2) the organizational structure which influences the process of making decisions; and (3) the values that are promoted within organizations, especially as these influence the content of decisions made by administrators.

## ORGANIZATIONAL LOYALTY

The proposed theoretical framework for administrative ethics assumes that the moral order of the society will be the dominant source of moral guidance, and also assumes primary loyalty to that society and moral order. Recently, it has been argued that loyalty to the society and the moral order is rivaled by a demand for loyalty to organizations. This type of loyalty could have significant implications for administrative ethics, and will be explored further.

Organizations provide many of the same kinds of behavioral cues as society provides (e.g., obligations, duties, norms and values). For that reason an organization might be thought of as parallel or comparable to a society. These parallels between society and organizations have led some to suggest that members of the organization have moved beyond merely working within an organizational structure and context, and have moved toward an "organizational citizenship" along the lines of social or political citizenship. Citizenship suggests that organizations have cultures that could influence the decisions of the administrator, and that the organizational culture will compete with the culture of the society in the mind of the administrator faced with a decision having important ethical dimensions.

The concept of organizational citizenship posits that "relevant citizenship experiences of modern man may be rapidly shifting from traditional modes of political affiliation" to organizational affiliations (Denhardt, 1968:47), resulting in significant shifts in commitments and sense of obligation. The importance of this observation for the study of administrative ethics is that in taking a position within a public organization, and becoming a loyal member of that organization, an administrator might be making a commitment to enhance and protect the organization along with its structure, authority patterns, and significant norms which have been developed in that organization. These are the organizational equivalents of the Constitution and social values which are most often thought to guide administrative behavior. Public administrators as "citizens" of organizations might be accepting obligations and loyalties that will greatly influence their ability to make ethical decisions in the broad sense of the term.

The kinds of obligations assumed by organizational citizens will vary somewhat depending on the organization in question. For example, "citizens" of the multinational corporation are described by Barnet and Muller in *Global Reach* as experiencing "nothing less than the replacement of national loyalty with corporate loyalty" (Barnet and Muller, 1974:89). For multinational corporations, the purpose of transcending national loyalties is to permit executives to move effortlessly from one nation to another and to be identified with the corporation rather than any particular nation. In other types of organizations, the rationale for encouraging organizational loyalty will be different but the overarching goal will be to overcome national (or even regional and local) differences among the members in order to enhance commitment to the organization and facilitate its goals.

Scott and Hart, in *Organizational America* (1979), explore the phenomenon of organizational loyalty through their discussion of the dominance of the "organizational imperative," and the effects it has on the individual. The organizational imperative is based upon the proposition that "whatever is good for the individual can only come from the modern organization. . . . Therefore, all behavior must enhance the health of such organizations" (Scott and Hart, 1979:43). It is suggested by Scott and Hart that, by continually acting on the assumptions of the organizational imperative, the individual will lose the ability to make independent judgments and to take personal responsibility for actions (rather than responsibility only as an agent of the organization). Individuals will also lose the ability to seek any good other than the good of the organization. Further, this shift in values suggests that "the values of *all* persons who influence the organization, whether from within or without, must be modified so that they complement the organizational imperative" (Scott and Hart, 1979:47). This "modification" of values results in the displacement of the values of the individual and the fundamental moral order.

This theme of organizational loyalty and a new organizational "ethic" has been addressed by many other writers. In Ralph Hummel's book *The Bureaucratic Experience* (1977), we find chapters entitled "Bureaucracy as the New Society" and "Bureaucracy as the New Culture." Robert B. Denhardt's *In The Shadow of Organization* (1981) critiques the all-encompassing "ethic of organization" that has come to dominate modern society, limiting individual autonomy and responsibility. Dennis Thompson wondered at the *possibility* of administrative ethics in organizations given the strong influence of the "ethics" of organizational life: the "ethic of neutrality" which "asserts that administrators ought to act neutrally in the sense that they should follow not their own moral principles but the decisions and policies of the organization"; and the "ethic of structure" which "asserts that not administrators but the organization . . . should be held responsible for its decisions and policies" (Thompson, 1985:555).

The theme is also evident in Terry Cooper's (1982) discussion of the obligations of the public administrator. He states that the "role as employee of a specific organization, although theoretically only an expression of one's larger public servanthood, is far more powerful and concrete in its sanctions and incentives" (Cooper, 1982:34). Cooper goes on to point out how, in the mind of the administrator, loyalty to the organization can become synonymous with upholding the public interest and result in a view that "carrying out the orders of superiors is tantamount to fulfilling one's duty as a public servant" (Cooper, 1982:34).

When organizational loyalty alone serves to define one's duty as a public servant, this represents a failure to understand the true rationale for organizational loyalty and obedience to authority. Loyalty to the organization is a legitimate part of ethical administration as it has been conceptualized here, because it is a responsibility that administrators have willingly undertaken and which benefits society. However, the individual must weigh that obligation against the myriad other obligations that should influence ethical decisions. Blind loyalty that fails to take into account other loyalties or obligations (such as loyalty to society and the moral order) is *not* considered a form of organizational loyalty that would contribute ultimately to ethical action for public administrators.

A variety of factors might lead to such blind loyalty. In assessing the organizational context of professionals and scientists, Dean Yarwood points out just how strong the influence and control of the organization is: "Formal organizations are among the most powerful social structures of our time, rivaling even the nuclear family in their impact" (Yarwood, 1985:482). Though it is certainly possible for administrators to choose *not* to be blindly loyal to the organization, and to instead choose to follow the values of society and the moral order, to do so often means considerable sacrifice, such as the loss of job, wages, and status associations (Denhardt, 1968:52).

Protecting one's career is not the only reason one might choose organizational loyalty over loyalty to the society and the moral order in a particular case. For example, the administrator might value highly the stated goals and objectives of the organization, and therefore choose to give precedence to the organization's needs over all others in order to enhance organizational success and survival, even though in a particular case protecting the organization allows social values to be violated. At other times, the individual might find it easier to accept the organizational perspective simply because it is more immediate and perhaps more clearly defined than the vague and conflicting interpretations of the moral order. According to the Scott and Hart (1979) argument, society permits such a displacement of values because the benefits of the modern organizations are themselves so highly valued that protection of those organizations justifies some sacrifice.

Thus, organizational loyalty taken to the extreme (which too often it is) has a clear impact on the ability of the individual to engage in ethical decision making. The ultimate impact of this loyalty displacement will depend on the degree of difference between the values dominant in the organization and the values which represent the fundamental moral order of the society. The greater the differences between these two sets of values, the greater the likelihood that administrative actions will be viewed as unethical from the perspective of the larger society.

There is reason to believe that the differences between behavior based on organizational loyalty and behavior based on loyalty to the society or moral order are considerable. Specifically, while efficiency, effectiveness, survival of the organization, and obedience to authority might be valued by society, they are not the predominant values. To the extent that these values are practiced in organizations to the exclusion of other social or moral values, the decisions made in organizations will not be the same decisions that would be made in other social contexts. Thus, analyzing administrative action within the organizational context can contribute significantly to the understanding of the current ethical state of public administration. The analysis might also reveal how much potential there is in using organizational change as a strategy for developing a more ethical public administration.

Administrators functioning within organizations are influenced by both structural and normative aspects of those organizations. The structural aspects of organizations tend to define the duties and obligations of organizational members, and in this way determine what problems administrators will see as theirs to act upon. The structure also influences the way in which administrators go about solving or acting upon the problems they face. The normative dimension will be examined in terms of the values and norms which are characteristic of modern organizations. Efficiency, effectiveness, reliance on formal rationality in decision making, and rewards based on technical competence are some of these norms and values. Emphasis on this value construct will affect the prospects for ethical administration in fairly dramatic ways.

While the argument that follows will be presented as if these structural and normative characteristics are equally descriptive of all public organizations, this is not the case. However, the characteristics (and tendencies toward those characteristics) are sufficiently widespread that all of public administration will benefit from serious reexamination of the potential impact of the stated characteristics on administrative action.

## ORGANIZATIONAL STRUCTURE

The bureaucratic organizations within which public administrators function have some fairly consistent structural characteristics: division of task based on functional specialization, hierarchical division of authority and control, and an elaborate and formal system of rules and procedures defining roles and methods of carrying out duties. The rationale for each of these characteristics is to either increase control over organizational members or increase the efficiency with which the member can carry out a job. But each also has some influence on the ability of an individual to act in an ethical manner (i.e., to be independent, deliberative, and critical in applying morality as a decision standard in organizational decision making). The interaction of the various characteristics forms the environment in which administrative action takes place, and this environment is quite powerful in limiting administrators' efforts to function ethically in many organizations.

Louis Gawthrop has argued that when the external environment of an organization becomes more complex than the expertise within the organization can absorb, the tendency is to strengthen organizational control mechanisms in order to shield out the increased complexity (Gawthrop, 1984:4-5). This strengthened control function reduces the choices available to administrators, and limits the capacity of the individual to be responsive to society and the moral order (i.e., to behave in an ethical manner). The structural characteristics of hierarchical authority, division of task based on specialization, and rigid rules and procedures, each serve that control function.

Others suggest that strong control mechanisms serve the needs of *individuals* as well as the organization. The thesis of the argument is that many people find the responsibility for making judgments too burdensome, and that as a means of protecting themselves they design organizations in such a way as to avoid that burden. Isabel Menzies (1960) studied nurses in a London hospital and found that the responsibility of making decisions regarding patient care was so anxiety-producing for them that the nurses developed an organizational structure which effectively protected them from having to make those decisions, or at least from making the decisions alone. She described narrowly defined tasks, elaborate checks and counterchecks, purposeful obscurity in the formal distribution of responsibility, and delegation of responsibility to superiors as some of the ways in which nurses reduced the anxiety associated with their jobs. Her description of the means for avoiding taking responsibility for making decisions parallels many of the characteristics said to describe bureaucratic organizations.

This raises the interesting question of whether individual preferences help explain some of the characteristics found in today's public organizations. Certainly there are jobs in public administration that are anxiety-producing and which might lead to such efforts to reduce responsibility. For example, social workers would be in very much the kind of situation faced by the nurses Menzies studied, and taking responsibility for those decisions would indeed be burdensome. In coping with that anxiety, social workers might be quite willing to engage in very narrowly defined jobs with rigid rules and hierarchical authority, but do so under the guise of maintaining organizational control and efficiency.

The question about whether these structural characteristics serve *organizational* purposes or organizational *members'* purposes is an important one. However, it will be deferred until Chapter 4 and the discussion of the individual. The more immediate task is to examine the structural characteristics of organizations in terms of the influence of such structures on administrative ethics.

## Division of Task Based on Functional Specialization

Tasks in bureaucratic organizations are typically divided in such a way that they are highly fractionated and relatively independent of other tasks. Such division is based on the assumption that efficiency results from functional specialization and simplification of tasks. The specialization tends to increase as organizations grow in size and complexity.

Division of tasks into functional specialities allows the organization to operate smoothly and efficiently, and allows the organization member to develop expertise within that narrow function much more quickly than if attempting to master a larger and more complex function. This same principle has been applied to the formulation of organizations as well—frequently a problem is not, or cannot be, addressed by just one public agency because each agency has its own area of specialization and expertise. The problem of children abusing aging parents for example, might be dealt with by several different agencies—the Division of Aging, Family Services, and Social Services—with no single agency assuming responsibility for the overall outcome of the interventions in the affected families.

This type of functional specialization is justified because the specialist develops a high level of expertise that is beneficial to the organization and to the society which is enhanced by the public service. This behavior provides the organization, society, and client groups with standardized practice, easily anticipated behavior and outcomes, control and security. Perhaps the organizational member is also relieved of some anxiety associated with taking moral responsibility for actions. On the other hand, such consistency, quality, and diffusion of responsibility comes at the expense of wider vision and individual judgment of the organizational participant which might be used to question organizational policy and procedures, and thus provide the necessary check on organizational excesses which can be exerted only by the individual finally performing a task.

High levels of functional specialization pose the risk that the relationship between the task being performed and the intended organizational objectives will become blurred. When this happens, organizational activities can become disjointed and organizational objectives might not be met. But perhaps more importantly, when the relationship between the task (means) and the organizational objectives (ends) is not visible, there is little basis on which to make either ethical or practical judgments about the task function. The isolated task loses its meaning, and its significance cannot be judged in terms of whether it meets organization objectives. It also becomes difficult to judge the task from a moral perspective since neither the intention nor the consequences of the action are fully understood. Thus, the moral issues will be difficult or impossible to identify.

Understanding the relationship of one task or decision to others, and anticipating outcomes or consequences of the decision are necessary in order to pinpoint the relevant ethical issues in a situation. Whether one takes a deontological or a teleological approach to judging the morality of an act, the extremely narrow perspective of considering one act or decision in isolation of all the related acts and decisions, is simply inadequate. An admittedly extreme illustration of this point might be asking a person assigned the task of turning on the gas in the chambers of Auschwitz to make a judgment about the morality of that act (turning a knob) in isolation of any consideration of the actions of others that brought hundreds of people into the chambers which the gas would fill. A less extreme example follows in Case 3.A.

### Case 3.A

An administrator in a large public housing agency has the job of keeping records of rent collections and making determinations about eviction for non-payment of rent. The administrator does not have responsibility for placing tenants in public housing, or any case work associated with the clients. Consequently, decisions about evictions are often made without consideration of the particular circumstances of the client since such information is not routinely available to the administrator. Sometimes this results in eviction notices going out to tenants who have experienced delayed welfare checks for an extended period of time, even though the delays were caused by improper actions or snafus in other parts of the welfare system, not through the fault of the client.

Clearly, the morality of the decisions just described cannot be adequately evaluated without knowledge of their relationship to the actions of others, and perhaps some knowledge of the expected outcomes. Yet, jobs frequently are structured in a way that their relationship to other tasks and to organizational purposes is obscured.

The rational model of administration, which provided much of the rationale for specializing and simplifying tasks, recognized that individuals have somewhat limited capacities in terms of gathering, processing, and utilizing information in the decision-making process. Organizations were believed to approximate true rationality by coordinating the efforts and capabilities of many individuals in order to accomplish a given task (Simon, 1948). To do this, however, tasks and major decisions were divided in such a way that often one individual could not be held responsible for a decision. When one is working on only a part of a task it is difficult to feel responsible for the success, failure, morality, or immorality of the task as a whole. While a task can be divided into parts it is much more difficult to divide ethical judgments into parts. All of this means that ethical deliberation is made more difficult by the very structure of the organization. Since the characteristic of highly fractionated tasks is so pervasive, both within and between organizations, any negative effects it has on ethical administration will be multiplied in intensity.

Perhaps, it might be argued, the coordinating and control functions of higher levels of management will adequately address the needed ethical judgments. In other words, ethical responsibility and accountability would be determined by, and accommodated by, the hierarchical authority structure of the organization. This argument will be explored in the next section.

## Hierarchical Authority Structures

In a system of hierarchically arranged authority, those at the lower reaches of the hierarchy have very little authority, and are responsible to numerous other levels of control. The result is that those at the lowest levels of the hierarchy have very little authority of their own and have a great deal of authority imposed upon them in the form of rules, directives, and systemic requirements that have been established either by those above them in the hierarchy, or which have become standard operating procedures for that organization. Clearly this pattern of authority severely limits the range of decisions to be made by those at the lower levels of the hierarchy.

Those at the upper reaches of the hierarchy have responsibility for, and authority over, the many subordinates below them in the organizational structure. One could conclude from this that top level administrators have the greatest amount of authority and that, at least at that level, the administrator would have enough authority, responsibility and information to comprehensively assess actions within the organization, and make ethical decisions about those actions. In other words, top administrators could make decisions about the ethics of organizational policies and procedures in a critical, moral and independent manner.

This supposition is called into question in a variety of ways, however. One recent study of high-level federal executives found that 26 percent agreed that organizational expectations "had sometimes required them to compromise their personal values" (Schmidt and Posner, 1986:452). The same study found that the behavior of organizational superiors was the most significant factor in contributing to *unethical* actions by managers. The authors suggested that the "distinction between personal and organizational values . . . often becomes blurred, especially the longer one stays with a particular organization and/or advances up the hierarchical ladder" (Schmidt and Posner, 1986:452). Therefore, while the authority of the top administrators might be sufficient to make and enforce ethical judgments, the critical independence necessary to make those decisions might have been compromised in the process of moving up the hierarchy.

Another study of federal bureau chiefs indicates that even at the highest levels of an organization, the potential impact of an administrator's exercised authority is severely constrained. Kaufman finds that two types of constraints exist which prevent bureau chiefs from controlling and influencing the bureaus as they would like: first, "the prior programming of the behavior of the bureau's work force," and second, "the imposition of agendas on bureau chiefs by events and conditions and people not under their control" (Kaufman, 1981:91). While the bureau chiefs can attempt to change the prior programming by issuing new rules and guidelines, the task is an immense one with constraints simultaneously being imposed from outside the organization.

The external constraints that Kaufman describes generally take the form of imposed agendas such as the regular budgetary process, the boundaries of routine understandings existing between the bureau and its constituents, and unpredictable but regularly occurring events such as changes in legislation, emergencies, and scandals (Kaufman, 1981:124-133). These events are constraints for the bureau chief in the sense that they take time that might otherwise be spent devising changes in the procedures and policies of the organization, and they impose limits on the kinds of changes that might feasibly be implemented.

In one sense the prior programming of the organization is very beneficial—those policies and procedures are what enable the organization to continue to function effectively in the temporary absence of an administrator or when the administrator is attending to the external environment. The external constraints in many cases will be beneficial for society by defining limits within which the top-level administrator may act. But, those constraints also mean that even the top administrator in an organization has somewhat limited control of the ethics, efficiency, and effectiveness of the organization, and placing all responsibility for the making of ethical judgments on the top levels of the hierarchical structure will be detrimental to the overall level of ethical behavior. In addition, with the proliferation of levels of hierarchy, and increasingly specialized tasks, even the administrator who manages many specialists may have authority over such a small part of the overall organizational function that it is difficult to assure ethical outcomes.

Two other scholars have examined the notion that the structure of authority within organizations could effectively address the relevant ethical problems of the organization without imposing ethical responsibilities on all individuals. Thompson (1985) described this as the "ethic of structure" and Stewart (1985a) outlined three arguments—role, systems theory, and executive accountability—which are used to ascribe moral responsibility to organizations rather than to individuals. Both Thompson and

Stewart reject those arguments on theoretical grounds and instead argue that individuals, not organizations or authority structures, must be held responsible and accountable for the morality of their decisions. When this does not happen, the ethical climate of organizations almost by necessity will deteriorate.

Thus, relying upon the hierarchy of authority to ultimately determine who is to make ethical judgments about the organizational programs, actions, and decisions will often result in *no one* being attentive to and making judgments about the ethical nature of organizational activities. The hierarchy has precisely the opposite effect: it allows and encourages organizational members *not* to take on that responsibility or exercise that authority at the lower levels of the hierarchy. And those who reach the top levels of the hierarchy might have lost the necessary perspective to make independent ethical judgments, or might be so severely constrained by "prior programming" in the organization that the decisions will be ineffective.

### Rules and Procedures

The third characteristic of organizational structure which is relevant to ethical administration is the elaborate system of rules and procedures that exists in bureaucratic organizations, much like Kaufman's "prior programming" described above. These rules and procedures prescribe for organizational members specific methods for completing tasks, boundaries within which to operate, decision rules to apply when faced with ambiguity, and even procedures for communicating with others in the organization.

This elaborate system of operating rules contributes to the control, consistency, continuity and efficiency needed in organizations. It allows members of the organization to act without stopping to deliberate over what should be done in each situation. But because no such deliberation is called for, there is little opportunity or reason for anyone to question the rules or think about the morality of their actions. The behaviors which will typically be reinforced are "going by the book" or following instructions of those in authority, because these are seen as appropriate loyal behaviors.

To the extent that the rules and procedures are moral, they will contribute positively to the organizational outcomes and to maintaining high levels of morality in organizational practice. If, on the other hand, the rules and procedures are morally questionable, the lack of critical evaluation contributes to immoral outcomes.

Moral and virtuous rules and procedures, which bureaucrats could follow with full confidence that they are fulfilling their obligations to society, the moral order, and the organization, do not occur by chance. Rules and procedures are developed by individuals in organizations, and the morality of those same rules and procedures will depend upon the deliberations of those individuals at the time of development. With careful thought given to justice, fairness, equity, and other moral principles, rules and procedures can be developed which could be followed in good conscience.

Such careful thought and ethical reflection are not often part of the rule-making process, but even carefully developed rules and procedures can have unintended consequences, or can be applied in an inappropriate way. For example, the rules and procedures might be designed to be consistent with, and to serve, the purposes of a particular profession which might be predominant in an organization, and not necessarily serve the greater public interest or the fundamental moral order. There is never a guarantee that the rules and procedures will be sufficiently "good" that they can be followed blindly over long periods of time. For that reason, viewing the ethical administrator as one who applies principles of morality to decisions and actions will contribute more to achieving moral outcomes in organizations than can be expected by altering the rules and procedures, simply because it insures that someone will be evaluating the rules and procedures after, as well as before, their inception.

Perhaps as important as the problematic issues that rules and procedures do address, are the problems and situations which are *not* covered. In such cases the organizational member must use discretion in making a decision because the rules and procedures do not clearly specify what is to be done. The evidence suggests that bureaucrats do practice considerable discretion (Rohr, 1978:26-40). However, in organizations where rules and procedures cover so many aspects of a person's job, there is often very little guidance for making decisions in the absence of rules. This ambiguity of discretion becomes particularly acute when the bureaucrats must also wonder whether it is within the realm of their task (job description) to act in this instance, and whether they actually have the authority to make a decision. Such uncertainty can be anxiety-producing and counter-productive because of overdependence on rules and procedures and too few opportunities to develop skills and confidence in making discretionary decisions.

It is significant that one of the major complaints about bureaucratic organizations is the "runaround" one gets when making a request which doesn't fall clearly within the existing rules or guidelines. In a related vein, a newspaper editorial suggested that, as a society, we are exhibiting "symptoms of advanced proceduritis," in which any issue raised quickly becomes a debate over *"how* the decision ought to be reached" (i.e., the "proper procedures") rather than *"what* the decision ought to be" (*Wall Street Journal*, 1983:30).

"Proceduritis" and the inability to make decisions without a rule book to refer to have a variety of causes, as previously described. The solution is probably not in getting rid of all the rules and procedures, but rather in giving individuals within organizations opportunities and the necessary skills to make the difficult decisions somewhat·more independently.

### Conclusion

In most bureaucratic organizations member roles are defined in a very narrow way due to the structural characteristics of organizations. Highly fractionated or specialized task functions require a fairly narrow range of responsibilities for the individual member. The hierarchy of authority and control narrows that range of responsibility even further. Finally, the elaborate system of rules and procedures narrows the range of decisions to be made even within the member's area of expertise and responsibility.

The clear message to organizational participants is to carry out their limited responsibilities in organizationally approved ways, and always in deference to authority structures. Expectations about ethical behavior are rarely expressed explicitly, and critique of rules, outcomes, or the decisions of others is not a part of the role definition at all. In fact, critique is often firmly discouraged as evidenced by the experiences of whistle-blowers (Truelson, 1986).

If the rules and procedures, control mechanisms, and task outcomes are reasonable and ethical, then few ethical problems arise as a result of a narrow role definition. But as mentioned earlier, such a situation is unlikely since almost every administrator will be participating in policy making as part of daily decisions, and good and ethical policies and procedures will only result from careful ethical deliberation. Unless every administrator's role includes responsibility for carefully deliberating over such decisions, many rules and procedures will not be ethically sound. What is likely to be *substituted* for ethical deliberation is an application of the individual's understanding of the norms and values of the organization.

## ORGANIZATIONAL NORMS AND VALUES

Just as bureaucratic organizations share many structural characteristics, so they share many norms and value constructs which will influence actions of organizational participants. These norms and values have evolved in order to serve organizational purposes, but will also have a dramatic impact on administrative ethics because organizational participants are likely to internalize, or take as their own, these values as a sign of their commitment to the organization. Then, when faced with a problem or decision, the behavioral norms of the organization will become a primary influence.

The framework developed in Chapter 1 assumed that the values that should guide administrative action would be those that make up the moral order of society. Yet, the values and norms that are typically present in organizations, and which often guide administrative action, are norms of efficiency and effectiveness, reliance on formal rationality in decision making, and rewards based on technical competence. These will be examined in order to determine how they influence the practice of administration and to what extent those norms interfere with ethical administrative action.

## Efficiency, Effectiveness, and Rationality

Efficiency and effectiveness are frequently the criteria used in judging programs, policies, and decisions in the organizational setting, and are accepted as among the most important goals in administrative practice (Schmidt and Posner, 1986). These norms, along with a reliance on formal rationality, reflect the broad influence of the scientific paradigm as well as a considered response to significant problems faced in the history of bureaucratic organizations. How they came about and what this means for administrative ethics will be explored in the following pages.

The norms of efficiency and effectiveness are in part a result of the early twentieth-century reform measures which set out to improve methods of staffing, organizing, and decision making by removing the favoritism and waste associated with the spoils system and replacing it with the merit system and bureaucratic organization. The reform measures are often thought of as responding to the problems of corruption on fundamentally moral grounds, but as Nigro and Nigro (1976) point out, while the crusaders of the reform movement leading up to the Pendleton Act clearly believed that the spoils system inevitably led to graft (and thus violated their sense of morality), they also "wanted the spoils system eliminated as a first step toward providing more efficient public service" (Nigro and Nigro, 1976:5).

Other reforms have also been pursued in the name of efficiency and effectiveness, including an increasing reliance on rational scientific analysis and empiricism. It was suggested that administrators should rely more on hard, empirical facts and scientific analysis in making decisions, in order to improve the capacity of government to serve its citizens and in order to enhance neutrality. This was seen as an improvement over the kinds of value-laden decisions, devoid of sufficient facts, which were perceived to characterize earlier public administration.

Using efficiency and effectiveness as measures for judging a program, action, or decision has considerable functional value, particularly if these measures can be quantified. These criteria emphasize the connection between the means (program, decision) and the ends (goals which are assumed to be clearly defined), and by formalizing the measures, discourage waste of the public's resources. But despite the laudable purposes of this type of rationality, the predominance of these norms in modern organizations has raised considerable ethical problems.

In his book *The Theory of Social and Economic Organization* (1947) Max Weber anticipated the kinds of problems that have arisen due to the changing norms of organizations. He describes the differences between "formal" and "substantive" rationality. Formal rationality is a system "in which the provision for needs . . . is capable of being expressed in numerical, calculable terms, and is so expressed" (Weber, 1947:185). Substantive rationality, on the other hand, conveys the notion that "it is not sufficient to consider only the purely formal fact that calculations are being made. . . . In addition, it is necessary to take account that . . . activity is oriented to ultimate ends . . . whether they be ethical, political, utilitarian . . . or of anything else" (Weber, 1947:185). What has happened is that formal rationality has become the dominant form practiced in organizations, while substantive rationality, with its parallel concern with "ends" or goals, has not.

The norms of efficiency and effectiveness (which can largely rely on formal rationality) are not in themselves problematic. In fact, applying these norms in making judgments about particular courses of action can be highly valuable and desirable, as long as those are not the *only* norms applied to such judgments. Therein lies the problem. Efficiency and effectiveness are norms which reflect the dominant force of instrumental rationality on modern organizations. In the mode of formal rationality—which is based on instrumentalism—a decision, program, or act can be judged as "good" only if it is efficient and effective, and was arrived at using the appropriate scientific method. No judgment about the morality of the goal of the program is made because in instrumentalism, the goal (or end) is taken as a given rather than as something the administrator has any influence on, or choice about. Because the goal is left for others to judge, instrumentalism or formal rationality judges only the *means* used in pursuit of the goal. Since the goal need not be judged, formal rationality (in Weber's terms) replaces substantive rationality, and moral standards are not applied.

The problem with pursuing exclusively the norms of efficiency, effectiveness, and instrumental rationality is that these norms were established at a time in public administration which is very different from what administrators now experience. The civil service reforms outlined for public organizations a role based upon the politics/administration dichotomy which assumed that the policies to be implemented by the bureaucracy were fully defined by the responsible elected body. In the ensuing years, the role of the bureaucracy has changed, moving toward a greater policy-making role. When administrators actively participate in decisions about "ends" (goals of policies) then instrumental rationality and the norms of efficiency and effectiveness are inadequate since these focus only on judging *means* rather than judging ends.

Not only is the instrumental rationality of scientific analysis inappropriate if used to judge the goals of policy decisions (because it is based on quantitative data rather than values), but it has had wider impacts as well. The increased use of empirical methods brought about great improvements in some aspects of public administration, but at the same time had the effect of separating value questions from questions of empirical fact. Ultimately, this had the effect of putting value judgments in a somewhat suspect and less legitimate category as a justification for an administrative decision. Perhaps because of the many positive contributions made by the use of empirical methods (e.g., increased efficiency and improved capabilities) few lamented the decline in use of value judgments as the basis for decisions, and many administrators moved away from consciously making value judgments in their work.

For those people trained in the skills associated with scientific analysis and rational technical competence, the consideration of ambiguous, ill-defined moral concepts may well seem like a step backward in the development of public administration. However, the renewed interest in administrative ethics is testimony to the fact that empirical competence is insufficient in the administration of public policy, and that incorporation of ethical principles is necessary. The technical achievements brought about by the use of scientific analysis based on instrumentality must not be ignored or underplayed, but the role that this trend had on the decline in legitimacy of value judgments and the decline of ethical deliberation must be taken into consideration as well.

While the civil service reforms and the increased use of scientific analysis were pursued both for functional *and* moral purposes, it was the functional aspects which in the end became the dominant focus. The functional dimensions eventually predominated because organizations were structured entirely along the functional dimensions, and the moral dimensions (assumed to remain with the individual administrator) were eventually lost as administrators began to express greater loyalty to the organization than to the social order. The functional norms of the organization, then, become more important than the social norms of ethics.

One cannot calculate, measure, or deduce moral concepts such as freedom, justice, or equality which need to be applied when making judgments about the ends or objectives of public policies. Thus, the type of reasoning which is predominant in modern organizations fails to incorporate ethical concerns in the decision-making process. For the administrator this means that in choosing an appropriate form of reasoning to achieve one set of values (efficiency and effectiveness), the implicit choice has been made to ignore other social values.

The problems associated with exclusive reliance on functional rationality are not limited to the administrative implementation of clearly immoral policies. A problem also arises when policies are only vaguely defined during the political process (as is often the case), leaving it to the administrator to make many decisions which in essence help define the "ends" of the policy as well as the means. Administrators trained in the art of efficiency and rationality do not automatically make the transition to a new method of reasoning given a different kind of situation, and they continue to apply the standards of efficiency and effectiveness even when making the policy choices necessary in such a situation. The problem, then, is not that efficiency and effectiveness are not important values to pursue, but that these values are used inappropriately in making judgments about the ends or objectives of the policy because administrators have not developed the type of reasoning skills necessary to make moral judgments about those policies. This approach is not only reinforced by the functional rationality of modern organizations, but by the reward systems as well.

### Rewards for Technical Competence

Reward systems in organizations are intended to reward and reinforce performance which helps achieve organizational goals, and to deny rewards for other types of performance. Thus, the reward system of an organization is likely to reinforce the pursuit of efficiency, effectiveness, and reliance on formal rationality in decision making because these behaviors help to achieve the goals of the organization. The organization is likely *not* to reward efforts associated with ethical reasoning such as questioning authority or rules, because these do not directly help in achieving the goals of the organization and often come at the expense of efficiency.

The reward system just described will tend to reward behavior which is "technically competent." "Technical competence" usually means that one acts in an efficient and effective manner as defined within the organization, and that one makes decisions based on formal rationality. Thus the organizational reward system will usually fail to give adequate consideration to moral issues and concerns because such issues are *socially* or individually defined, and are not within the definition of technical competence which is of primary concern to the organization.

Organizational reward systems encourage loyalty to the organization, obedience to organizational authority and rules, and strongly encourage identification with the organization. In order for the organizational participant to receive the valued rewards (jobs, promotions, status, recognition, pay, etc.) the individual must exhibit behavior consistent with those demands. If the rewards controlled within the organization are valued highly and are not available elsewhere, the organizational participant is likely to behave in the manner deemed acceptable within that organization. Persons who fail to exhibit acceptable behaviors (and thus fail to receive rewards) will tend to either change their behavior or to leave the organization for one which rewards the kind of behavior they do exhibit. Thus, the organizational reward structure as described is very effective in reinforcing the primacy given to technical competence, but does so at the expense of reinforcing administrative behaviors which focus on ethical inquiry or the application of moral principles to administrative decisions.

The ethical ramifications of this situation are that the organizational participant is likely to suppress personal and social values when those conflict with the norms encouraged within the organization. As Hummel (1977) argued, the bureaucrat will take on an organizational personality which is different from the personality exhibited in a social context. When making decisions within the organization, then, the bureaucrat is likely to adopt decision rules that are acceptable in the organizational context but which would not have been the decision rule employed by the person in a social context. Ethically positive behaviors such as questioning the morality of instructions and assignments given, critically evaluating the outcomes of tasks, and applying decision rules such as equity, justice, or the maximization of freedom, will be avoided. Those who engage in these behaviors will tend not to receive the rewards available within the organization because such activities will at times come at the expense of the appearance of the efficient and effective use of resources and the apparent loyalty to the organization.

## CONCLUSION

As has been argued, the organizational environment of most public administrators is not conducive to the practice of engaging in ethical deliberation. The structural characteristics in many ways discourage situations from arising in which ethical deliberation would be likely to take place. The norms and goals found within the organization are such that the member who allows those norms and goals to inform discretionary decisions is more likely to receive valued rewards than would the member who instead engaged in ethical deliberation and made decisions based on moral concerns.

When approaches to ethics such as those suggested by Rohr (1978) and Cooper (1982) are practiced within existing organizations, the ethical administrator is not likely to be rewarded in the usual ways, and will find that they are in violation of standard practice in the organization. As evidence, witness the experiences of many whistle-blowers (Bowman, 1983a; Truelson, 1986). In order for any approach to ethical administration to be workable, the norms, structures, and expectations of loyalty within organizations must be adequately addressed within any proposals dealing with the problem of public administration ethics.

The role of the organization in public administration ethics has been acknowledged and addressed by other authors (Boling and Dempsey, 1981). Suggestions for institutionalizing ethical inquiry and for protecting those who practice ethical inquiry are a part of these proposals. Unfortunately, neither the individual approach which gives administrators the necessary skills for engaging in ethical inquiry, nor the organizational approach which institutionalizes the inquiry will be adequate to the tasks of increasing the level of ethical inquiry in public organizations. It will be necessary to combine both of these approaches—the individual and the organizational—in order to arrive at an acceptable and practicable approach to improving ethical decision making in public organizations.

# 4

# THE PATH TO A MORE ETHICAL PUBLIC ADMINISTRATION: THE INDIVIDUAL

Having suggested both social/historical and organizational pressures that interfere with ethical deliberation and decision making, the task now is to outline ways in which the practicing administrator can more directly follow the model of ethical administration that is implicit in contemporary discussions of administrative ethics. Various criticisms of administrative behavior were outlined as that model was developed, and addressing those criticisms will require reconciling the ideals expressed in the model with the realities of administrative practice, and suggesting any necessary reforms which might be needed to enhance public administration ethics. The reconciliation and suggested reforms will need to target both the individual administrator and the organizations within which those individuals function, and should result in a framework that administrators could reasonably and legitimately follow, and organizations could reasonably accommodate. This and the following chapter will focus on those targets.

It will perhaps be useful to restate key elements of the model: the ethical administrator is one who examines in a critical and independent manner the standards by which decisions are made, attempting to reflect the morality of society as well as acting in consideration of the administrators' commitments, obligations, and responsibilities to the organization, and to other individuals and groups to whom the administrator is accountable. Applying this model to the practice of administrative ethics requires that the *domain* of the administrator's ethical focus be outlined; the *content* of acceptable and applicable moral standards must be defined, and a *process* for deliberation over competing values must be described.

Within any discussion of domain, content, and process issues, the many constraints on administrative practice must be recognized and accommodated. Those include: (1) societal constraints on the administrative role, including the need for administrators to maintain public confidence and to be held accountable to the public; (2) structural and normative organizational constraints—perhaps the central challenge to administrative ethics; and (3) the possibility that individuals seek to avoid taking moral responsibility for their administrative actions, thus resisting any efforts to encourage ethical deliberation and judgments. These constraints will be addressed in each of the following sections.

## THE DOMAIN OF ETHICS IN ADMINISTRATION

How can public administrators define what they are ethically responsible for, and to whom they are responsible? Dwight Waldo attempted to answer this question by sketching a "map" of ethical responsibilities as shown in Figure 4.1.

Terry Cooper made a similar effort when he discussed the "Objective Responsibilities" of administrators (to the laws governing the organization, to the hierarchical structure of authority in the organization, and to the public interest) and the "Subjective Responsibilities" of administrators (to values, attitudes and loyalties arising out of experiences with family, friends, schools, religious affiliations, professional training and organizational involvement) (Cooper, 1982:43-55).

**Figure 4.1**
**Sources and Types of Ethical Responsibilities**

The Constitution                                    Nation
Law                                                 Democracy
Organization-Bureaucratic Norms                     Profession
Family and Friends                                  Religion or God
Public Interest or General Welfare                  Self
Middle-Range Collectivities (e.g. party, class, race)
                        Humanity or the World

Source: Dwight Waldo (1980:103-106)

In a different context, but one very related to defining the domain of ethical responsibilities of administrators, Robert Goodin (1985) argues that dependency and vulnerability give rise to moral claims on those to whom or upon whom one is dependent or vulnerable. He says this is true not only of familial relationships where we readily accept the notion of such special responsibilities and moral claims, but of public life and matters as well. His argument focuses on an ethical defense of the welfare state, but could clearly be applied to many client groups who are dependent on the government, to taxpayers who are dependent on administrators to spend their tax dollars wisely and efficiently, and even to fellow members of an ethnic or gender group who depend on the good job performance of one of their members to open up further employment opportunities to that group. Goodin's argument would lead us to conclude that the domain of ethical responsibilities for the administrator would be very broad, since there are many individuals and groups who are dependent on or vulnerable to the public sector, and who would consequently make moral claims on the administrator.

Others have suggested that administrators also have the often overlooked responsibility for questioning inadequate or unethical legislation rather than merely implementing it, and for helping to produce ethical legislation. As Kenneth C. Davis, an expert in administrative law, noted:

The attitude is that as long as the injustice is caused by the statute, the administrator has no reason for concern. One major responsibility of every agency . . . is to watch for deficiencies in the legislation it administers, and to make systematic recommendations for changes. . . . Administrators must share the responsibility for producing legislation that is sound, workable, and just. . . . (Davis, 1969:53)

Beyond this, an administrator has a responsibility to carry out all administrative duties (not just policy related duties) in an ethical manner. These other duties would include, but not be limited to, supervision and peer review. In order to fulfill these expectations regarding ethical behavior, the administrator must subject a wide range of actions and decisions to ethical scrutiny and deliberation.

How can all of these sources of obligation be taken seriously into account in defining the domain of ethical responsibilities for the administrator? Some have argued that the domain is really much narrower than just described—that it has been intentionally narrowed by the political system (which has at times embraced the notion of a politics/administration dichotomy); intentionally narrowed by the chosen mode of reasoning and analysis (which has at times embraced the notion of a fact/value dichotomy and instrumental reason); or intentionally narrowed by organizational structures (which at times embrace the notion of rigid hierarchies of authority and narrowly defined tasks). Each of these arguments has been put forth as a reason that administrators are not responsible (ethically or otherwise) for many decisions, actions, and policies.

All three arguments have been addressed, and refuted, in previous chapters. The politics/administration dichotomy has no basis in reality where administrators are involved in the setting of policy agendas, and where a review of several policy implementation studies leads the authors to agree with Michael Lipsky's statement that "the latitude of those charged with carrying out a policy is so substantial that . . . policy is effectively 'made' by the people who implement it" (Nakamura and Smallwood, 1980:19). No mode of reasoning, including scientific analysis and instrumental rationality, is without value biases which must be put to the test of ethical deliberation. And finally, though organizational structures surely are intended to limit the authority and responsibility of organizational members, this cannot be interpreted as relieving members of the ethical responsibility for their actions (Thompson, 1985; Stewart, 1985a).

The evidence can suggest no other conclusion: the domain of ethical responsibility for the public administrator is very broad and very encompassing. Administrators are intimately involved in the policy-making process, the analyses they use in arriving at decisions have ethically relevant value biases, and organizational structures do not relieve individuals from responsibility for the actions, policies, and decisions in which they take part.

This conclusion is for the most part accepted in the field of public administration. It is important to say "for the most part" because there are those who agree that administrators are involved in the policy-making process and have broad discretionary powers, but who see the potential arena of administrative decision making as entirely too broad, and lacking a requisite degree of legitimacy. They urge efforts to remove some of the opportunities for making value laden policy decisions, thus narrowing the domain of responsibility for the administrator. We will explore some of their concerns and suggested reforms.

Discretionary authority for administrators seems to be increasing as legislatures fail to reach a clearly articulated policy agreement, thus necessitating the delegation of broad discretionary authority to the administrators who implement the law (Lowi, 1969). Lowi argues that such delegation undermines principles of accountability and responsibility by putting policy-making authority into the hands of unelected officials, and suggests that there needs to be movement back toward clear legislative mandates and centralized policy-making authority.

Kenneth C. Davis expressed similar concerns about the consequences of the increasing amounts of discretion given to administrators: "Where law ends, discretion begins, and the exercise of discretion may mean either beneficence or tyranny, either justice or injustice, either reasonableness or arbitrariness" (Davis, 1969:3). He goes on to say that "the greatest and most frequent injustice occurs . . . where rules and principles provide little or no guidance, where emotions of deciding officers may affect what they do, where political or other favoritism may influence decisions, and where the imperfections of human nature are often reflected in the choices made" (Davis, 1969:v). He proposed that because of these problems with administrative discretion, discretion should be structured and checked whenever possible in order to achieve the desired just outcomes: "Structuring includes plans, policy statements, and rules as well as open findings, open rules, and open precedents. . . . Checking includes both administrative and judicial supervision and review" (Davis, 1969:55).

Both Lowi and Davis are concerned that the bureaucracy is playing an extensive governing role without being held accountable through elections, and that the administrators are governing in an unethical as well as unchecked manner. Clearly the question of governance without accountability is a serious concern, which is precisely why the ethical use of discretion is such a central part of administrative ethics. Experience tells us that administrative discretion sometimes does lead to injustice and other undesirable outcomes. However, it is not necessarily the case that the injustices result from moral failures of administrators. There may be alternative explanations such as that administrators have not interpreted their role as policy critic broadly enough, or that the procedures and constraints in the organization discourage ethical decision making. Another possibility is that the administrator would make better judgments if provided with more direction and guidance as to appropriate moral content in those judgments.

The kinds of severe restrictions on administrative discretion that have been suggested by Lowi, Davis, and others reflect a view that administrators should be entrusted with discretion only as a last resort. Davis sees the necessity of administrative involvement in the policy process, but gives the impression that administrators can make a contribution to the policy process only when there is no way to reasonably make policy at another level, and only when their discretion is limited, structured, and checked.

This perspective, it will be argued, does a disservice to public administrators by showing too little confidence in the judgments of those administrators, and provides too narrow a view of how administrative discretion can be guided in order to contribute to ethical outcomes. Additionally, narrowing the discretion of administrators may make it more difficult, rather than less difficult, for them to act in an ethical manner and to exercise their responsibility for making independent moral judgments. But to ignore the concerns that prompted these proposals for limitations on discretion would lead to an inadequate model of administrative ethics. Therefore, a closer look at the arguments and proposals (especially Davis') will serve the development of a sound model for ethical administrative action.

Davis recommends that the standards guiding discretionary decisions be defined and publicized in a manner similar to the administrative rulings of the Securities and Exchange Commission and the Internal Revenue Service. In this way the discretionary decisions of individual administrators will gradually lead to the development of rules (based on precedent), which are then used to decide future cases (Davis, 1969:21). This leads to the gradual replacement of discretionary decisions with rules (or administrative law) to be publicized and followed by other administrators. In other words, the discretionary judgments made by one administrator become rules for another. There is considerable value in this—public disclosure of the standards applied in making decisions will provide opportunities for challenge and critique, and will encourge administrators to make judgments that can withstand such scrutiny. In addition, those decision standards which hold up best under public scrutiny might lead to the development of a set of principles that could be used to guide all administrative action. One would hope that those decision standards would include moral principles as well as criteria such as efficiency and effectiveness.

The problem with this approach, though, is that the discretionary decisions made by one administrator might become a "rule" for others, but the process of critique and public scrutiny might never have occurred. There is no guarantee in this process that any person or group will engage in the necessary ethical deliberation. When the decision of one administrator becomes a rule for the next, then what develops could be characterized as a new type of rigidity that restricts discretionary authority (and the domain of ethical responsibility) in a different, but not necessarily better, way. In fact, this process could potentially lead to the institutionalization of bad policy.

Restricting administrative discretion does nothing to reform its practice (the real concern of those who call for such restrictions) and therefore might be a self-defeating effort. Davis' view is that the undisciplined practice of administrative discretion has led to a less just society, so he proposes structuring, and thus restricting, that discretion. But, a more just society is not likely to result unless ethical deliberation over the initial decisions becomes a mandatory, and regularly practiced, part of the process as well. Davis seems to assume that such deliberation will occur, but experience tells us such an assumption is risky.

We are suggesting a different approach which is more likely to meet with success in addressing the basic concern about administrative discretion and the very broad domain of ethical responsibility for administrators. This approach might be more effective because it: (1) helps administrators develop the necessary skills for using the discretion in an ethical and reasoned manner, and (2) holds them accountable on those bases. Such an approach would call for administrators to make reasoned and principled contributions to the policy process, and to make other administrative decisions which can withstand both moral and rational criticism. This approach would ensure that administrators have some guidance as to the appropriate process for engaging in the public debate of decision standards, and guidance as to the appropriate moral content for critiquing those standards.

Administrators who follow a sound process for arriving at a decision about public policy and who make the judgment based on decision principles that are justifiable, will not only be able to withstand ethical inquiry, but will also be making positive contributions to ethical public policy outcomes. Administrators can be held accountable for this broad set of responsibilities only if these expectations are clearly defined. The remainder of this chapter will attempt such a definition by addressing the questions of acceptable and applicable moral *content* in administrative decisions, as well as questions about a *process* of deliberation over competing values.

At this point it should be said that the discussion will contain a bias toward relying on the existing abilities of individuals to make ethical judgments. This is seen as preferable to reliance upon complex methods of arriving at decisions which are not only impractical but which also give the impression that individuals cannot rely on their own judgment in making administrative decisions. Such avoidance of the individual's judgment might alleviate some immediate and short-term concerns about the quality of those judgments, but in the long run serves only to excuse the individual from making any kind of ethical judgment, as the process is both impractical and alienating. Instead, a framework that provides guidance and constraints for individual judgments will be proposed, one which makes use of individual moral consciousness and creativity rather than relying upon complex procedures preordained by some authority outside of the individual administrator.

## THE PROCESS DIMENSION OF ADMINISTRATIVE ETHICS

In suggesting that the domain of administrative responsibility is extremely broad and encompassing, concerns are undoubtedly raised about whether such a broad domain is consistent with the abilities of administrators to meet the demands of ethical action. As stated in the beginning of this chapter, if the proposed model of administrative ethics is to be applied, a more complete description of the process of ethical deliberation must be presented. The first element of the process of ethical deliberation to be addressed will be the question of the critical analysis of decision standards—what should be subjected to critical analysis and how such critical analysis can be done. Next will be a discussion of individual responsibility, and how this differs from reliance on a process of decision making based on organizational position. Finally, there will be a discussion of the process of applying values in rational decision making, which is important because any ethical decision-making process must accommodate the mode of reason most familiar to practicing administrators.

## Critical Analysis of Decision Standards

In developing the field of administrative ethics it is important to clearly delineate expectations that administrators are to critically examine the morality of their actions and engage in ethical deliberation. This involves determining whether or not the standards used in making their decisions are moral, and determining which of a set of competing values should be applied to a particular decision. Such determinations are expected at the very least in all cases where the administrator is exercising discretionary authority, and at most in evaluating all decisions (even those which simply follow the directives of a legitimate higher authority).

In a previous section we addressed the "domain" question of why such broad areas must be submitted to ethical deliberation. Now we turn to the process of carrying out such critical analysis. One difficulty that immediately arises is the *recognition* of decision standards. Public administrators often follow rules and regulations made by others, and decision rules which take the form of organizational standard operating procedures (SOP's). Since the administrator did not develop the rules and the SOP's it is difficult to recognize what decision standards are at work even though these decision standards contain implicit value choices and will directly influence the ethical practice of administration. For example, assumptions or decision premises guide the formulation of computer programs and are value laden, but the use of such programs in making decisions is rarely subjected to close moral scrutiny. Similarly, decision premises become subsumed in the standard operating procedures of organizations, and are difficult to recognize as important ethical concerns. But a failure to examine those assumptions will have significant moral implications, and therefore these must be included in a framework for administrative ethics.

In addition to making use of decision standards, many administrators also create decision standards for others to follow. In either role (as creator or user) similar skills can be applied.

These skills involve examining the value assumptions in decision standards and using ethical premises in justifying the decision standards. Another skill often required will be establishing priorities when two or more values or moral principles conflict with one another.

In order to fulfill these expectations, the individual must be able to: (1) identify decision rules and policy objectives, (2) determine what the values and assumptions of those decision rules and policy objectives are, (3) critically assess the ethical foundations of those value assumptions, and (4) make an ethical judgment about the situation. For reasons discussed earlier, one of the most difficult of these to put into practice is the identification of decision rules and policy objectives, but the other steps are also problematic as shown in Case 4.A.

## *Case 4.A*

When social welfare agencies had the rule that AFDC (welfare) would be denied to any household in which a man resided, the decision standard was clear, and the reasons for the rule seemed obvious and unquestionable: a man present in a household would be able to financially support that family without government assistance. A more probing look at this assumption reveals several underlying assumptions, such as: a man will be able to find work should he desire to do so; a man by his mere presence has an obligation to support the people living in the household, regardless of his relationship to them; and, finally, the welfare agency has the right to explore the personal and family situation of those seeking assistance. The Supreme Court did not find all of these underlying assumptions completely defensible and struck down the "man in the house" rule.

Opening decision standards and underlying assumptions to ethical inquiry leads to the question of how to engage in that kind of critical analysis. In making a judgment about the morality of the outcomes of such a decision standard, it is important to ask questions such as: Does this rule violate any basic moral principles? What impact will this rule have on those to whom it is applied? If the answers to those questions reveal that the affected individuals will benefit in the long run (or at least not be harmed), and that no basic moral principles are violated, then the decision rule might be morally justifiable. If the answers reveal that the rule might contribute to the breakup of poor families (as in Case 4.A), or that a fundamental principle such as justice or liberty is violated, then a different judgment might be made. This example is indicative of the delving into decision standards which administrators and others (not just Supreme Court judges) must do if they are to contribute to ethical public administration. It also indicates the kind of difficult choices that are involved in administrative ethics—in this case, a choice between the right to privacy of the client and the public's rightful expectation that welfare dollars be used in the most efficient, effective, and reasonable manner possible.

For the practicing administrator this process requires developing observation and questioning skills needed in order to identify the decision premises and values in operation. Skills related to analysis of the moral content or moral principles involved are also needed, perhaps requiring some knowledge of the various approaches to understanding the moral order. In addition, administrators need the ability to make justifiable choices among conflicting moral principles. For the most part, these skills are ones which individual administrators practice daily, either in their professional or private lives, and the main new challenge will be conscientiously applying them to a more broadly defined set of ethical concerns.

Since all decisions and actions, regardless of how small and insignificant, rest on unseen assumptions or decision standards, the task of identifying those standards is an onerous one. The importance of it should not be underestimated, but on the other hand, administrators should not be placed in a position in which they feel they must always explore the full range of assumptions before taking any type of action. That would be the ideal situation, but is clearly impractical. Therefore, the administrator should develop a set of priorities that helps in identifying the situations in which assumptions and long-term ramifications should be explored before action is taken.

Typically, *new* policies and procedures will need to be singled out for examination, as will policies that can lead to significant changes in the life chances of individuals or groups. More broadly, Douglas Yates suggests that determining whether policies deserve careful value analysis will depend on "whether they (a) cut close to certain main public values and (b) have substantial policy implications" (Yates, 1981:45). New policies simply provide an ideal opportunity for such questioning. Policies that are irreversible or that significantly alter life chances of individuals have a very high priority because they affect individuals in such a way that they take on significantly greater moral importance. But all policies should be closely examined, especially if they enter unexplored public realms or are in areas in which previous actions have been largely unquestioned and standardized.

Precisely because some procedure has "always been done this way" and is so fully accepted might be a good reason to choose that decision standard for critique. It is quite possible that the decision standard is not as defensible as it appears, or if it is defensible, a great deal can be learned from its evaluation.

The ideal remains that all decision standards should be subject to such criticism, but practical implications require that priorities be established, and the brief guidelines just presented offer some guidance in priority setting. The priorities can be adapted to the particular situation of the administrator and the types of decisions and tasks which are carried out in the organization. Also, if such a process of ethical critique has been a part of administrative practice for some time, a set of policies, SOP's, or decision standards might have developed that would serve as adequate rules or precedents for future administrative action, without an immediate need for further critical review.

Ultimately, the individual administrator will be required to make the judgment about which policies, procedures, rules, and decisions should be critically analyzed, and when this should be done. It must also be left to the administrator's own judgment to determine when the decisions or judgments of others should be called into question. No matter how elaborate the guidelines or codes of ethics we develop, there is no way to separate the individual judgment of administrators from the development of a more ethical public administration. The impetus to act in an ethical manner, in the final analysis, comes not from external guidance, but from taking individual responsibility for one's actions.

### Individual Responsibility

In taking individual responsibility for administrative actions, an administrator must be willing and able to make independent judgments about ethical issues. In other words, the administrator must be able to critically evaluate the situation and its moral implications. This includes critical evaluation of the views or practices within the organization, of peers, and even accepted societal values when necessary. This type of independence is necessary in order to prevent the administrator from implementing immoral policies which appear to have the legitimacy of proper authority and social acceptance. Individual responsibility rests on the premise that no outside authority or structure can give *a priori* justification for any course of action; instead the individual must take responsibility for determining whether such a justification exists.

For example, racism was socially accepted in many predominantly white communities, and Jim Crow laws had the legitimacy of legal authority. Ideally, though, those who were charged with implementing those laws would be able to make a moral judgment about racism independently of that apparent legitimacy and acceptance. Going against accepted practice is very difficult and many administrators will not have the desire, ability, or confidence to make such unpopular judgments about the policies they are charged with implementing. But if a framework for ethical action is to encompass the whole range of ethical dilemmas that administrators face, the framework must allow for the possibility that the administrator will make a judgment about a situation which is different from that of peers, organizational superiors, and even from what the community would make in that situation. At times, only by making such independent judgments and taking the associated risks, will progress toward a better society be made.

This is not to say that the administrator should ignore the

resulting impact on the organization, or ignore the various other obligations incumbent upon the administrator—these are also important ethical considerations. But it does require that the administrator be willing to step back from those constraints and obligations and look at a situation as an independent moral being. This differs in only subtle ways from what other authors have suggested for the ethical public administrator, and the difference lies in the degree of independence involved.

The approach being suggested here goes beyond assuming that the administrator is above all a keeper of regime values as Rohr (1978) suggests, or that the administrator can make ethical judgments by recognizing and acting according to the various roles and responsibilities the administrator has as a citizen and member of an organization, as Cooper (1982) suggests. Both of those approaches constitute important considerations for the ethical administrator, but in the final analysis it is the obligation of the administrator to make an independent judgment about the morality of the situation. This view is consistent with Kohlberg's (1969) theory of cognitive moral development in which the highest level of moral development is one in which the individual is able to make independent moral judgments, but does so in light of known obligations to others.

While it is possible to give the administrator some guidance as to what the appropriate moral principles ought to be, it is not possible to give such specific guidelines or to develop a sophisticated enough process for arriving at moral judgments to assure that the administrator will not have to rely ultimately upon an individual moral judgment. In a democratic society where majority opinion typically rules (or carries great weight), this aspect of the ethical framework might be criticized as allowing the tyranny of minority opinion. But, to expect administrators to judge the morality of actions or policies according to majority opinion (or accepted social practice) would be to erode the very concept of morality by equating morality with what "is" rather than what "ought to be." In addition, to expect administrators to make judgments in this way also gives the tacit message that, indeed, the individual is not personally responsible for the morality of actions, rather the responsibility rests with the society as a whole to give the appropriate messages to the individual. This shift in responsibility makes moral accountability more difficult to enforce.

The expectation that administrators should accept personal responsibility for all of their actions and decisions is not a new theme in the ethics literature. However, in terms of being considered an integral part of administrative ethics, the concept took on new importance as writers such as Wakefield (1976) argued that the internal control associated with individual responsibility offers a much more effective solution to ethical problems than do institutionally based controls. Most approaches to administrative ethics focus on enhancing institutional controls either through precise rules such as conflict-of-interest legislation, or through more subtle mechanisms of tying ethics to specific obligations (such as to one's superiors). This seems to represent a reluctance to rely on the individual's judgment about right and wrong. But institutional controls cannot adequately serve as a substitute for individual judgment, and movement in that direction seriously hampers efforts toward increasing accountability.

Another problem often identified with an emphasis on individual responsibility is its practical applicability, given the working environment in which administrators function. That environment is such that organizational tasks are fractionated, giving each individual only a part of the task to perform; authority is ordered in such a way that the administrator may have very little authority to do anything other than what is instructed by administrative superiors; and taking individual responsibility for one's actions may be interpreted as compromising one's organizational loyalty. Evidently, there are many aspects of the organization that will discourage the taking of individual responsibility, but those organizational hindrances will be discussed in the next chapter. First, we will explore how the individual administrator can go about accepting and retaining individual responsibility in even the most discouraging of organizational environments.

The concept of "individual responsibility" clearly indicates that the person taking such responsibility does so as an *individual*. By implication this means that the *position* held by the person does not become the repository for the responsibility, nor does any other person, regardless of his or her authority or power over the individual who is making the decision. Too much emphasis being placed on the responsibilities of the position, or the responsibilities of the administrator to others, will detract from the importance of individual responsibility as the foundation of administrative ethics. The ramifications of such a shift in focus away from the individual are important and have been recognized as one of the contributing factors to the failure to develop a more ethical public administration.

As for the position becoming the repository for responsibility, this raises some very difficult issues, some dealing with the meaning of the organizational role, some with the responsibilities of that role, and some with the difference between public and private morality. The administrator is placed in a position of making moral judgments because of the organizational role, and therefore that role has a significant impact on the perceptions of and about the administrator. This could lead the administrator to behave in a way consistent *not* with individual morality but, instead, consistent with perceptions of what is expected of the position held. Case 4.B describes such a separation between individual morality and the position.

### Case 4.B

During a time of severe budget upheavals during the Reagan administration, many proposals for cutting social service programs were put forth, coming mainly from a bevy of economic advisors to the President. Those advisors felt that their positions as *economic* advisors required that they make those difficult decisions in the interest of the impact on the economy, rather than in terms of any impact on individuals. When confronted with examples of the suffering of individuals which resulted from the implementation of these cutbacks, one of the economic advisors was reported to have said that he could not do his job if he thought about the impact of his decisions on individuals. Clearly, the responsibilities to the *position* were separated from the responsibilities to individuals, and there was a sense that having fulfilled responsibility to the position alleviated responsibility for the outcomes of the decisions, at least in the mind of that particular economic advisor.

A viewpoint such as that expressed by the economic advisor in the case indicates that the advisor could not reconcile the demands of his position with his own moral principles. This supports the view of Menzies (1960) that individuals might create organizational structures and norms that help them avoid the anxiety associated with the judgments they must make in their work, and avoid the responsibility associated with those decisions. Thus, organizational structures and norms might be as much a result of individual preferences as they are a result of efforts to achieve efficiency, effectiveness, and control. Individual responsibility as a basis for an ethical framework will meet considerable resistance if this is the case. The difficulty of taking that responsibility is not sufficient justification to allow avoidance of the responsibility, but it does increase the importance of education, training, and institutional support mechanisms in the effort to enhance the ethical tenor of public administration.

Case 4.B does raise a very important issue: the role that one's position within an organization should play in influencing one's ethical judgments. Moral outcomes cannot be expected if approaches to ethical administration encourage separation of moral individuality from organizational position. On the other hand, the economic advisor has no easy answer, even if he maintains his moral individuality in making his recommendations. The issue here is a choice between the necessity of cuts in the federal budget in order to serve the public interest (assuming that large federal deficits are not in the public interest) and making cuts in social programs which are also considered morally valuable and in the public interest. One could argue that these represent conflicting obligations—obligations to the taxpayer or the nation as a whole to responsibly manage the budget, and obligations to the individuals served by the social programs.

If the economic advisor acknowledges only the obligation to the taxpayer (because that more accurately reflects his organizational position), then he will probably not give adequate consideration to the moral obligations to the social program recipients. If he considers only the responsibility to the recipients of government assistance, then he is not acting responsibly toward his obligations to efficiently manage the budget.

The model of administrative ethics that has been outlined

here insists that he must consider both sets of obligations rather than focus on one and ignore the other. The economic advisor is ethically obligated to manage the budget efficiently (perhaps based upon the moral principles associated with his promises when he took the position, or perhaps on the basis of a principle of fairness to the taxpayer), but in doing so must give adequate consideration and weight to the needs of, and obligations to, recipients of social programs.

This point of view does indeed make the job of the economic advisor more difficult—these are very difficult choices to make—but only in the sense that he must now *consciously* make a choice about what he had before implicitly chosen by failing to consider the impact on individuals. He might decide that the social programs can be cut justifiably without doing undue harm to the participants, or he might decide that social programs cannot be cut justifiably and that spending cuts must come from other areas of the budget. In either case, the decision must include consideration of the full range of moral implications and this can only be done if the economic advisor does not attempt to narrow the range of considerations by defining obligations only in terms of organizational position.

It has been recognized that there are special cases when the position held by the administrator requires that personal codes of conduct (private morality) be violated in order to meet a public good such as national security (public morality). These cases are fairly rare, however, and should be exceptions to, not the foundation of, administrative ethics.

A very important aspect of individual responsibility is that it implies that there are others to whom one is responsible. Vickers (1965:14) suggests that by responsibility we are really referring to a construct of rules within which decisions are to be made, and though we may find that conflicting decisions could be made in a particular case, we would probably find that we all agree as to whether the decision was made responsibly (i.e., within the construct of rules). What this implies is that responsible administrative action necessitates acting within an accepted range of behaviors and actions, utilizing a construct that has been generally (though tacitly) agreed upon, thus structuring the options among which the administrator must choose.

The advantage of considering "responsibility" as a construct of rules is that it frees the administrator from perceiving that there is only one "responsible" thing to do in a particular situation. Many times we use the term "responsible administrator" in such a way as to imply that being responsible means doing that which the requirements of the organizational role necessitate. Using Vickers' concept, acting responsibly means that one acts within certain constraints on behavior, but those constraints are *considerations* rather than dictates of decisions, and the constraints are broadly defined, not limited to one role of the administrator (in this case, not limited to the organizational role and obligations).

This discussion helps point out that while the individual ultimately must take responsibility for a decision, the individual is not responsible only to self, but to many things and people outside the self. The domain of ethical responsibilities discussed in the previous section shows how extensive the responsibilities are. The delineation of a construct of responsibilities, though, does not provide the moral guidance necessary for judging among those various obligations. In addition to making the "responsible choice," the administrator must also make the "ethical choice," which requires applying moral consideration as well as responsibility consideration to the judgment. Only in this way do the individual's powers of reason and judgment as well as individual moral convictions come fully into play.

As noted earlier, there are powerful organizational forces that will discourage the administrator from making ethical decisions in an individually responsible manner. Perhaps the most significant source of discouragement will come from pressure to make decisions based on instrumental rationality *to the exclusion of* moral considerations. Administrators must make decisions that give due consideration to the values of efficiency and effectiveness, because that constitutes part of their range of obligations. However, these values should not be adhered to exclusively, causing a failure to give adequate consideration to other values—and too often this is precisely what happens in administrative practice because of too much emphasis on quantifiable variables, and too little emphasis and guidance on being an ethical administrator. In order for the administrator to integrate the ideals of ethical behavior with the realities of organizational life, there must be an effective integration of morality and rationality so that the influences on administrative decisions are not in direct conflict with one another.

## The Meeting of Morality and Rationality

Empiricism, the administrative role, and individual decision-making capacities all have one common factor: all three relate to our use of reason. Empiricism has somewhat limited the type of information to be considered in the reasoning process. The administrative role, as it has come to be defined, has limited the scope and focus of what is to be reasoned about and by whom. And the capacity of the individual to make decisions without benefit of organizational assistance has been questioned (Simon, 1948). The whole concept of reason in administrative practice has come to be so restricted that it has virtually excluded questions of moral principles as they can and should be applied in the administration of public policy. In other words, ethical deliberation is no longer a part of the reasoning process so often prescribed for administrators (i.e., instrumental rationality). At best, ethical deliberation is a separate issue from the normal decision-making considerations, and at worst ethical deliberation is considered unnecessary or undesirable. As Davis put it,

When we isolate what we regard as the exercise of discretion, we find three principal ingredients—facts, values, and influences. But an officer who is exercising discretion seldom separates these three elements; most discretionary decisions are intuitive, and responses to influences often tend to crowd out thinking about values. (Davis, 1969:5)

As described in Chapter 3, formal rationality is predominant in organizations, usually to the exclusion of substantive rationality which would evaluate ends as well as means, or the bases of value judgments as well as judgments about instrumentality. Thus, for rationality and morality to meet in the practice of administration, the broader concept of substantive rationality or subjective reason must supplement the narrowness of instrumental reason in administrative decision making. Of course, we would not want instrumental rationality to be avoided entirely since the values of efficiency and effectiveness, and the contributions of empirical analysis which are associated with that mode of reasoning, are very important to administrative practice. But, that mode of reasoning should not be used to the exclusion of subjective reason which is associated with ethical considerations—there is a need for both types of reasoning, but as Weber pointed out, substantive rationality permits evaluation. of *both* means and ends, so encompasses as well as surpasses formal rationality (Weber, 1947).

In order for the practice of administrative ethics to be furthered, then, the broader concept of subjective reason must be incorporated into administrative practice, and the usual practice of allowing outside influences and intuitive decision making to crowd out consideration of values must be overcome. Part of the process dimension, then, is to make value considerations as intuitive as instrumental types of reasoning have become.

Perhaps one of the reasons that value judgments are not readily incorporated into administrative decision making is that arriving at ethical decisions requires a greater tolerance for ambiguity than does arriving at decisions based on empirical evidence alone. The nature of ethical dilemmas is that they are rarely black and white issues and rarely have measurable standards to apply to making choices between competing alternatives. Ethical judgments are inherently more ambiguous than judgments made about scientific facts. That does not mean, however, that there are no methods of dealing with the ambiguity of ethics, and incorporating a search for ethical understanding with a search for facts. Once again the philosophical traditions which are too often neglected can be of tremendous help in working through these difficulties. In this case, the work of Hannah Arendt on "judgment" shows a way of thinking about ethical reasoning that helps reduce the ambiguity.

To Hannah Arendt, the human faculty of "judgment" is not simply a reflection of the individual's self-interest and personal biases. She argues that "the power of judgment rests on a potential agreement with others . . . finds itself always and primarily . . . in an anticipated communication with others with whom I know I must finally come to some agreement" (Arendt, 1961:219–221). Thus ethical judgments might be thought of as something more than the process of applying personal moral convictions to public decisions, which would be suspect. Instead (borrowing from Arendt's work), ethical judgments could be thought of as resulting from a process of gathering information about the moral views of those with whom one must finally come to an agreement, and arriving at a decision which one finds personally acceptable, morally reasonable, as well as potentially acceptable to those significant others.

Gathering good information about others' views of moral principles can be done in a wide variety of ways, some of which have already been suggested in the administrative ethics literature. John Rohr (1978) proposed that searching through Supreme Court opinions on relevant cases would help the administrator gain a better understanding of the morality of our society. Boling and Dempsey (1981) suggested that organizations develop programs of normative enrichment in which individuals are informed of the value orientation of their peers and superiors in the organization, and share in the development and reform of ethical standards within the organization. These, and a wide variety of other processes, could be used by rationally oriented administrators in seeking some form of empirical verification that moral principles are important, and arriving at a better understanding of how others have applied these moral considerations in their decisions. This not only uses familiar data-gathering skills, but also requires administrators to be attentive to those with whom they must ultimately reach some agreement.

In order to deal with the ethical limitations of empiricism, administrators must recognize the legitimacy and necessity of incorporating nonempirical considerations into their decision-making process. Increasing the reliability of their nonempirically based judgments might be done by seeking out the opinions of relevant others and using this information in formulating their administrative judgments. The concept of subjective reason would encourage expanding the variety of sources consulted rather than seeking to limit or to define "one best source" of ethical guidance as some writers in the field of administrative ethics have tended to do.

In order to move toward the exploration of questions of purposes and ends (ethical questions), administrators will have to more broadly define their roles, obligations, and responsibilities beyond that which is currently prescribed in formal organizational structures. By broadening their focus to include not only efficiency and effectiveness, but also questions of efficiency and effectiveness *toward what end*, administrators will begin calling upon subjective reason. The point here is not that administrators should not seek to be efficient and effective. Efficiency and effectiveness are important social (and organizational) values, but they must not be used as decision standards to the exclusion of moral principles.

In an effort to bring the empirical and ethical dimensions of the administrator's job together, Fischer (1983) stated that "it is reasonable to surmise that the methodological success of the forensic model ultimately rests on the elaboration of rules that govern the exchanges between empirical and normative perspectives . . . " (Fischer, 1983:20). He then outlines an alternative decision model that integrates facts and values, developed from the informal logic of practical reason. The model guides the administrator through a series of questions of both normative and rational (empirical) content and thus helps the administrator to bring together both the rational and moral dimensions of the job, an approach "based on rigorous normative methods, but . . . anchored to the realities of public administrative discourse" (Fischer, 1983:16).

In summary, the ethical administrator must make decisions in a manner consistent with the obligations of morality as well as obligations of rationality. The two are not inconsistent with one another and can be effectively integrated in administrative practice, given a commitment on the part of the administrator and the organization for that to occur. One way of assuring that such a commitment exists, and that values are appropriately guiding administrative decision making, is through the process of holding administrators accountable for their decisions. This is the last area of the *process* of administrative ethics that will be explored.

## Accountability, Ethics, and Public Administration

A concern raised by Lowi (1969) about the extensiveness of administrative discretion was that it undermined accountability in the political process. In exploring this concern we find evidence that holding administrators accountable for their decisions is not such a difficult problem because the processes and mechanisms of accountability are very well-developed (though underutilized), and applying the mechanisms to ethical accountability will not be significantly different from applying it to other aspects of administrative decisions for which the mechanisms are currently used (e.g., efficiency, waste).

In fact, experience indicates that administrators are already held morally accountable for their decisions when there is an extreme violation of accepted moral standards. For example, after the explosion of the space shuttle *Challenger*, administrators and engineers were not held accountable only for the technical failure, but also for the morality of the decision to place astronauts at such risk over such a period of time. Thus, it will only be necessary to expand the existing accountability channels to consider the ethics of administrative action, and in this way contribute to the overall improvement of ethical administration in the public sector.

Bernard Rosen in *Holding Government Bureaucracies Accountable* (1982) describes how bureaucrats are held accountable by the elected chief executive, the legislature, citizen groups, the courts, and the news media. He suggests that these channels of accountability address moral issues as well as effectiveness issues with regard to bureaucratic activity. He concludes that "if a government bureaucracy is out of control, clearly it is not for any lack of means of holding it accountable and reining it in" (Rosen, 1982:159). But, he also concludes that the groups responsible for assuring that accountability are not living up to their responsibilities.

Kenneth J. Meier (1979) also came to this conclusion. In exploring the efforts of legislatures, chief executives, courts, and citizens, to control the bureaucracy, he finds that the means of control exist, but that there are severe weaknesses in the actual control. For example, he finds that the legislature fails to adequately control the bureaucracy because:

Legislation has become too vague to be more than a general boundary on bureaucratic action. The budgeting process tends to be incremental rather than control oriented. The legislative veto reduces Congress to responding to bureaucratic initiatives. Oversight offers too few rewards to Congress and casework introduces harmful favoritism in the administrative process. (Meier, 1979:154)

A model of bureaucratic/legislative relations put forth by Bendor et al., (1985) offers some hope that accountability of the bureaucracy is more effective than the incidents of oversight activity might suggest. The model suggests that because agencies do not wish to risk being penalized by Congress for inflated budget requests, monitoring by Congress "does not have to be perfect, or even nearly perfect, to have a disciplining effect" (Bendor et al., 1985:1056). The same is probably true of other avenues of accountability as well, so the pessimism about the lack of bureaucratic accountability may be exaggerated.

However, the failure of other groups to adequately hold administrators accountable gives further support to the argument made by Wakefield (1976) and mentioned earlier, that internal controls offer a more effective solution to ethical dilemmas than do institutional controls. Therefore the primary emphasis in administrative ethics should remain on developing the capacities of the administrator for making ethical decisions. However, institutional controls would be useful as a complement to this kind of individually centered activity. One important, though often overlooked, method of influencing ethical administrative action is through the organization.

## THE MORAL CONTENT OF ADMINISTRATIVE ETHICS

· Administrators can all too easily find sources of rules that will suggest the process by which to make a decision, but they are provided with few concrete suggestions about the content of the values to be applied in the deliberation process (i.e., providing concrete moral guidance). Most writers avoid making statements or suggestions that appear to be moralizing or that directly suggest values the author believes ought to be followed. Such avoidance is perfectly understandable when any attempts to make recommendations about appropriate moral standards are met with responses like Thayer's statement "I often have the feeling that those who most loudly proclaim the need for 'moral standards' really are seeking authority for themselves" (Thayer, 1982:17–18). It seems that taking a moral stance or expressing moral convictions is unpopular, at least among academics if not among practitioners. Such an aversion to explicit morality leaves little room for wonder why most of the administrative ethics literature dwells on the process of ethics and not on the content, and why the discipline has failed to develop a morally grounded code of ethics (Chandler, 1983b). It also helps explain why public administration as a discipline suffers from a credibility gap when it purports to be serving the public interest but instead falls into the patterns of instrumental rationality which ignore many dimensions of the public interest.

The more writers in the field of public administration ethics attempt to avoid making statements of moral principles, the more likely it is that administrators will get the implicit message that whatever decision they make is acceptable so long as they use the appropriate methods and terms in justifying it to others. This is the ultimate pitfall of moral relativism as discussed in Chapter 2. While it is highly desirable to avoid pointless moralizing, it is also highly desirable that administrators know what is expected of them in terms of the morality they are to put into practice. Failure to provide this guidance gives the administrator no alternative but to use personal moral convictions or rely on instrumental rationality to the exclusion of considerations of the public interest or social morality as it can be known.

Cues as to appropriate moral content of administrative ethics can be found in a variety of places in spite of the avoidance of explicit moral statements. For example, they will probably receive cues from the social issues which are of growing importance. Those issues represent the emerging value priorities of

the society and will become relevant aspects of the value construct which administrators will be expected to consider in
making ethical decisions. Of course, even though particular
values may have increasing importance in society, that does
not necessarily mean that the administrator must accept those
values as ones that should guide actions; it only means that
they are relevant for consideration, and that the administrator
is increasingly likely to be held accountable for having applied
those values in the decision-making process. Such was the case
during the 1960's and 1970's with the emerging social issues of
civil rights and women's rights. Administrators were becoming
increasingly accountable for the equity of their actions.

The administrator must make certain individual judgments
about whether the emerging social values are right and acceptable, and that responsibility must not be underestimated. The
administrators who found themselves in Germany during Hitler's rise to power were faced with what must have seemed to
be an emerging social value that called for discrimination against
Jews. In hindsight we can recognize that the value was in fact
wrong, but that is a difficult and lonely decision to make as an
administrator charged with some aspect of implementing that
concerted discrimination process.

The specific values which administrators would find in
emerging social concerns are such values as equity, freedom,
justice, fairness, and various individual rights. Today, issues
such as reverse discrimination and comparable worth are helping to delineate views about equity as a social value. Individual
rights are being addressed in issues such as a patient's right to
die, parents' rights to refuse medical attention for their children, and the emerging "fetal rights" controversy. These social
concerns will eventually find their way to the Supreme Court,
but the observant public administrator can gain a great deal of
insight into moral principles by analyzing these issues and then
developing a framework for applying those moral principles in
administrative decision making. The Supreme Court opinions
might well be useful educational devices, but administrators
need not wait for the Supreme Court to act before addressing
the moral issues in their own work.

During their academic training many administrators may have

been exposed to the democratic theory literature and to some exploration of the Constitution. These could provide the administrator with some guidance as to what is particularly relevant to this society and form of government (e.g., the various freedoms and rights specified in the Constitution, and the value underpinnings of democracies such as the right to a voice in government, as well as broader concepts such as natural rights). From this, administrators can understand better the larger construct within which they are expected to operate. Most administrators will do this implicitly simply because of long years of socialization in this society, but a conscious reexamination of those value underpinnings will reinforce their importance for the administrator and become a more important consideration in daily activities.

During the past decade, many efforts have been made to develop codes of ethics for public administrators. These codes came about primarily as a reaction to corruption during the Watergate era, but have also represented an attempt to provide some structure for the discretion which is a part of administrative life. For the most part these codes deal with issues of conflict of interest and clear cases of rule violation, and give relatively little guidance in terms of the application of social values in making the administrative decisions required of them. A 1981 survey of state codes of ethics revealed that while thirty-seven states were listed as having a "code of ethics," in only ten states did that code go beyond the typical conflict-of-interest list of prohibited acts (Hays and Gleissner, 1981:53).

Despite these shortcomings, administrators can learn something from these codes about the construct within which they are expected to act as public administrators. An exploration of these codes of ethics and conflict-of-interest laws will provide administrators with guidance for some of their actions, and guidance as to some social values. For example, the conflict-of-interest laws strongly suggest a social value that the individual should not unduly financially benefit from public service, which can also be interpreted as valuing the public interest over self-interest.

Codes of ethics provide broad cues as to important social values—honor, integrity, honesty, responsibility, and others. The codes fail to be sufficiently specific about the practice of those values, but nevertheless provide the administrator with general guidelines within which to make administrative decisions. With sufficient training in making moral judgments in administrative roles, and with sufficient authority to carry out those decisions, perhaps there is no need to be more specific in the codes of ethics, only a need to be more attentive in holding administrators accountable on moral grounds.

Beyond the very broad cues of the Constitution and democratic theory, beyond keeping up with changing social values, and beyond codes of ethics, the administrator still has a large area to explore. The "values clarification" strategies which are utilized in many ethics courses are important because they will at least make students and administrators more aware of the underlying assumptions and values that guide their daily decisions and the decisions of others. However, simply clarifying existing values is insufficient for the individual, just as identifying social values is insufficient. Identification of existing or practiced values in no way guarantees that those values are appropriate or right. Identification is an important first step and some useful values clarification strategies have been developed and are available for use in the classroom.

After having identified the existing or emerging social or individual values, the next step is to evaluate those values in terms of other standards of right and wrong. One possibility is to measure the emerging or existing values against the larger constructs discussed before—the Constitution, democratic theory, and various other philosophical traditions. If there is a conflict among the constructs, then this is an important area for ethical deliberation, and the individual administrator along with others must explore that conflict or dilemma and ultimately make some judgment about which set of values should be given priority or should be accepted as decision standards. Sometimes this may mean that the prevailing social norms or values will have to be violated in favor of the Constitutional or democratic values, and vice versa. Perhaps even more difficult would be for an individual to question established *personal* values in light of potential conflict with underlying social values contained in the Constitution or in democratic theory. This would be a difficult task and one that many administrators might wish to avoid, but such exploration and challenge to move beyond "values clarification" should be encouraged at some point in the administrator's early career, perhaps during professional education.

Finally, there are many religious and cultural value constructs that could be used to guide the administrator in making judgments about particular decisions, about the morality of social or individual values, and in trying to identify the construct of rules by which decisions are likely to be judged by colleagues, elected officials, constituents, and the public. Regardless of whether these constructs are clearly delineated for the administrator prior to the decision, they are nevertheless the general boundaries within which the decisions will be judged as reasonable, responsible, and acceptable. The greater the understanding the administrator has prior to such judgments by the public and others, the more likely it is that the administrator will have made both an ethical and a defensible decision.

The issue is not just that the individual be able to defend a decision, but that the decision also be one that is consistent with ethical considerations of the society and the individual. This allows not only the administrator to have some guidance in making decisions but also allows society to have some role in the structuring of administrative discretion and some expectation of the realm within which administrative decisions will be made. This would allow for necessary levels of consistency, but also avoid unnecessary and undesirable rigidity and mindless rule following.

There may be some questions raised about the possibility that administrators will each be seeking their own sources of guidance in ethical decision making and that this might result in administrators each being guided by a different set of ethical considerations when making decisions and critiquing the decisions of others. This will to some extent be the case. The individuals involved could be expected to consult sources of guidance most consistent with their existing value constructs and their preexisting modes of decision making. In other words, those individuals who have had a strongly religious background are much more likely to seek ethical guidance from that source than would someone with no religious leanings. At the same time, those who are more academically or philosophically oriented will seek guidance from those sources. The likely outcome will be that those who consult different sources for guidance will come out with somewhat different constructs or relevant values.

This is a problem only if absolute consistency and conformity are the desired outcomes. As argued earlier, consistency and conformity can be more detrimental to ethical outcomes than positive, if that conformity leads to noncritical rule following. Having a variety of sources of ethical guidance being consulted by administrators might lead to a much more well-developed ethical deliberation process than would otherwise be possible.

If the decision standards used by the administrator are publicly announced and critiqued, then true ethical deliberation would be the norm, and more formal rules and guidelines might be developed which could serve to inform administrative conduct in the future. Thus, the content dimension of public administration ethics would be gradually developing, while the process dimension will serve as an ongoing function to help resolve value conflicts.

While in the end administrators must rely on their own conscience in making a moral judgment, there is likely to be widespread agreement in the judgments of different people. After all, the individuals involved begin from a fundamentally similar value construct since most will have been socialized in this culture. In addition, the process of accountability will keep in check any serious discrepancies in judgment.

# 5

# THE PATH TO A MORE ETHICAL PUBLIC ADMINISTRATION: THE ORGANIZATION

A recurring problem encountered in the discussion of ethics and public administration is that some of the ethical problems and dilemmas faced by public administrators occur not only within their organizations but at least in part *because* of their organizations. Throughout the discussion of "the individual" in the previous chapter, it was noted that some ethical problems are brought about by characteristics associated with large, bureaucratic organizations. One example would be the failure to consider value implications of instrumentally rational decisions, because making value judgments is not an organizationally sanctioned activity. Another example would be the structure and authority patterns in organizations that can make it difficult for the individual to act in an ethical manner. Indeed, the policies and procedures within the organization might have the unintended, but very real, consequence of encouraging unethical behavior among organizational members.

If we are to have a more ethical public administration, organizations must be influenced in such a way that ethical behavior becomes legitimized, rewarded, and encourged. Another approach is to influence the professional norms of public administration, including socialization that occurs in the training of public administrators.

In a sense, the reform of professional norms bridges the individual and organizational approaches. When professional norms and socialization patterns influence the values of the administrator and thus influence administrative decisions, it is an "individual" approach. In addition, being a "professional" within an organization implies a set of roles and obligations for the individual that extend beyond the organization and the position. When professional organizations or associations develop and enforce codes of ethics or rules of conduct (such as in the professions of engineering, city management, law, and medicine), they are providing the individual with a system of norms, procedures and reward structures which can serve as a competing influence to the employing organization. Yet the source of this competing influence is distinctly "organizational."

How employing organizations influence the ethics of administrative behavior, and what types of reform efforts might enhance positive organizational influence will be the focus of discussion in what follows. In the course of that discussion some attention will be given not only to the problems and reform efforts of employing organizations but also of professional associations as well.

## ORGANIZATIONS AND ETHICS

While the bulk of attention of those dealing in the area of administrative ethics has focused on the individual, there are some who have suggested that the *primary* focus of administrative ethics should be on organizational reform rather than on individual reform. Boling and Dempsey (1981) present that argument as follows:

a different approach—one with more realistic prospects for long-term success—is to focus not on individual public administrators, but on the organizational settings in which they work. It is an approach which asserts that if we wish to improve the ethical tenor of organizational life we must devote our attention to a restructuring of the organization itself. (Boling and Dempsey, 1981:13).

This particular point of view is probably a reaction to the failures of past reform efforts that focussed only on the individual. While pointing out an important and often neglected element of administrative ethics (the organizational setting), Boling and Dempsey probably go too far toward the other extreme. A failure to direct reform efforts toward the individual *at the same time* as one develops reforms for the organization can result in a situation in which the new or reformed institutional arrangements serve as substitutes for the individual moral conscience, rather than as a method of encouraging ethical decision making.

Substituting institutional arrangements for individual moral judgments can have some serious consequences, as will be shown in this chapter, but for a variety of reasons is still a tempting approach to ethics reform. One reason is that individuals can be uncomfortable making ethical judgments in their work, and devising institutional arrangements which allow them to avoid those judgments can ease that responsibility. The inadequacy of institutional reforms as a substitute for individual ethical judgments is an issue that must be addressed. But so too must we recognize that individual reform without institutional reform can lead to a stalemate in which good intentions on the part of the administrator cannot be translated into action given the existing organizational arrangements. The better approach, then, is to attempt simultaneous and complementary reforms of the institution and the individual. The individual administrator must be given appropriate training and encouragement to act in an ethical manner and to supplement (or reinforce) this training, the organization must be reformed in order to accommodate and encourage ethical action.

It is assumed here that organizations can be reformed or changed in a manner which encourages members to make independent, critical, and moral judgments, without sacrificing the achievement of other organizational purposes. The basis of this assumption is that ethical action is expected by society, just as efficient and effective governmental operations are expected, and that efforts to make actions more ethically defensible need not detract from the traditional organizational goals of efficiency and effectiveness. Others, however, do not necessarily share the assumption that organizations can be reformed. That opposing viewpoint, as expressed in works such as *Organizational America* and *The Bureaucratic Experience*, will be examined.

### The Possibility of Organizational Reform

William G. Scott and David K. Hart (1979) in *Organizational America* believe the only hope for reforming organizations and transcending what they called the "organizational imperative" is that professional people within organizations (mostly middle managers) will lead a major reform movement aimed at restoring the individual imperative as the basis on which decisions are made, replacing the organizational imperative. The "individual imperative" is that *"all individuals have the natural right to the realization of the full potentials of every stage of their lives; therefore, all institutions must be predicated upon that right"* (Scott and Hart, 1979:226). Scott and Hart are pessimistic that professionals will actually lead such a reform effort, but nevertheless accept it as within the realm of possibility (Scott and Hart, 1979:220–223).

Ralph Hummel (1977) in *The Bureaucratic Experience* is even more pessimistic than Scott and Hart. Hummel suggests that "the public and its legislators, accustomed to the immense variety of complex services that bureaucracy does render, are no longer capable of rejecting the human cost that bureaucracy imposes as the price of rationalistic means of control" (Hummel, 1977:202). He argues that organizational life must be accepted as a different culture, calling upon the individual to act in a manner different from social norms. "The best we can do is to admit we are caught up in the process of rationalization and have recourse to whatever humanizing elements still possess the public's social and political imagination to moderate the extremes of bureaucratization" (Hummel, 1977:202). That recourse might be to become reactionary—acting slowly where bureaucracy promises speed, creating production lags where bureaucracy promises efficiency.

These writers present a view which suggests that organizations and instrumental rationality have become too dominant a force in our society and that the results are detrimental to society, organizational members, as well as clients of the organizations, even though there are important and recognizable benefits derived from organizations. Both books cite examples of unhampered bureaucratic power being used to the detriment of society and conclude from those examples that within organizations individuals no longer function within a socially accepted value framework. Instead, they suggest individuals are complying with an organizational value framework that places too much emphasis on efficiently and effectively meeting organizational needs (e.g., the needs for an orderly hierarchy of authority, a system of rules, or the priority of organizational survival) and too little emphasis on examining the social and value consequences of actions.

Hummel described the following case as an example of organizational needs taking precedence over needs of society and individuals.

*Case 5.A*

A corrections officer received a call from his elderly mother asking to be taken to the hospital. The officer requested permission for time off and the personnel manager denied the request because it would cause a shortage of personnel. (Hummel, 1977:65)

Denying the request was in the interest of the organization, and perhaps even necessitated by rules or guidelines mandating certain staffing levels. The case is problematic, though, because it seems the personnel manager was considering only the needs of the organization and not the value choice implicitly associated with the decision—placing the organization's temporary needs before the needs of the individual, which in this case might be a life and death situation. Cases such as this make clear the need for a new look at the balancing of organizational needs and the needs of society or the individual in making administrative decisions. What such cases cannot answer, though, is whether such a balancing of views is best achieved through individual or organizational reform efforts; or, if Hummel and others are correct, whether such reform is possible at all.

Those who see no hope for reforming organizations offer gloomy predictions about the future of a society in which individual and social values do not serve as the foundation of organizational action. This is in interesting contrast to those who see large organizations as no more than a neutral force in the lives of people, and therefore in no need of reform—the basic assumption of most ethical reform measures that focus on the individual to the exclusion of the organization. Which of these views is closer to reality?

It must be acknowledged by all who are interested in administrative ethics that the organization is not a neutral force on the actions of administrators. The organizational context, institutional operating procedures, and patterns of control all serve to limit the latitude within which an administrator can make decisions (Rizzo and Patka, 1981:107). The reward structures, budgeting procedures, and even discipline procedures can also serve to encourage unethical behavior. Therefore the organization as an institution must be a strong consideration in any reform effort to bring about a more ethical public administration. It would follow that if there really is little hope of reforming the organization, then there is little hope of improving the ethical tenor of public administration. This is a position that few would be willing to accept.

Organizations are structures, patterns, and rules which are created to meet the complex needs of people in society. Those structures, patterns, and rules are intentional and goal oriented (at least at the point of inception). Organizations are designed to meet some social and human needs, and are typically expected to do so in an efficient and effective manner. From time to time the ethics, reasonability, or advisability of activities engaged in by organizational members are questioned and criticized. The point that unethical conduct occurs in organizations is undeniable, but the question of how one interprets the situation is crucial to the development of administrative ethics. If one assumes that the unethical activity or conduct is inherently and unavoidably part of organizational life as Hummel, Scott, and Hart seem to imply, then the organization as an institution is open to the kind of critique given it by those authors, and is an unlikely candidate for reform. If, on the other hand, one interprets this as a situation in which, given certain conditions, the administrator could have made another (more ethical) choice, then the organization can be viewed as a powerful and productive institution in need of reform, rather than as a powerful but morally destructive force in our society.

The alternative viewpoints can be applied to Case 5.A: why didn't the personnel officer consider the value implications of the decision made? Scott and Hart might respond by arguing that organizations don't encourage the raising of value questions because it brings up "thorny questions about the worth of modern organizations. Thinking about values demands an intellectual and spiritual boldness that is not integral to the training of good managers" (Scott and Hart, 1979:4). Hummel responded by suggesting that "conflicts between individual human needs and systems needs are unavoidable . . . When such conflict arises, the tendency built into the system is to put the system first" (Hummel, 1977:66). Perhaps those are accurate explanations of the "system" as it has developed, but there might be another explanation for the failure to raise value questions.

Such failure might be a result of too narrowly defined tasks and overly centralized authority patterns which do exist in organizations but which might have been more inadvertent than planned. Narrowly defined tasks and very limited authority were design choices made in order to bring about greater efficiency and fewer opportunities for corruption in public organizations. In pursuing that direction, public organizations were designed in such a way that each person can achieve high levels of efficiency and effectiveness directed toward the goals attributed to the organization—in some cases very laudable goals meeting very real human needs. At the same time each person sees such a small segment of the overall organizational activity that moral judgments about those actions are often difficult to make.

Thus, the same reform efforts that gave us greater efficiency, effectiveness, consistency, and control also created a situation in which inappropriate actions or decision rules can go unchallenged. This was an inadvertent result of our own intentional reform measures. Interpreting the situation in organizations as unintended consequences of reform efforts allows for the possibility that members of organizations can pursue other courses of action and that organizations are open to the possibility of reform. In other words, we might argue that those who have authority in organizations can and will consider reforms designed to accommodate value choices as well as maintain acceptable levels of efficiency and effectiveness, because those reform measures will allow the system to perform efficiently and effectively but will also allow it to be more in accord with the moral order of our society. Thus, it *can* be argued that organizational reforms can be used to enhance individual reform efforts in administrative ethics, but it will be a challenging process, which will be described in the remainder of this chapter.

## THE OBJECTIVES AND NATURE OF ORGANIZATIONAL REFORM

First, it is necessary to outline the objectives for reforming organizations. The primary objective is to create an environment that will contribute to, rather than detract from, a reasoned and principled dialogue about organizational outputs and outcomes, and the behavior of organizational members. This dialogue must acknowledge not only our need for the organization or system to operate efficiently, effectively, and with some level of certainty, but also our individual needs to develop and express ourselves and our values in the course of public service.

Such expression is important not only for the organizational member but for society in general because the expression and consideration of values in the practice of administration permits the type of responsiveness to human needs that we expect of those in public service, and also prevents the perversions allowed when organizational activities are not subjected to value judgments. Achieving a reasoned and principled dialogue will require more informed critique of organizational practice, the use of reason that goes beyond instrumental rationality, and taking morality seriously in organizational life.

There is a second objective in pursuing organizational reform—to make changes within the organization which will find the proper place for organizational goals within an ethical structure. Ethics and efficiency should not be separated because one or the other is likely to suffer. There is a need to develop and recognize that pursuing efficiency, effectiveness, and economy are not ends in themselves, but are valued because they are instrumental in serving social purposes by enhancing organizational goals, and are also valued in an ethical sense because of the responsibilities of organizational members to achieve the purposes and fulfill obligations entrusted to them. As the code of ethics of the American Society for Public Administration indicates, it is an ethical obligation to use funds efficiently because we have been entrusted with that responsibility, and because the stewardship of public resources is valued.

Some of the very problems which detract from making ethical decisions also detract from making decisions in a timely and coherent manner. If some tangible benefit to the functioning of the organization (such as improved efficiency) can result from the reforms intended to improve the ethical tenor of organizations, then the reforms are more likely to be adopted.

Given this objective of linking ethics with traditional organizational values, we might also take one step further and explore ways that ethics might actually enhance organizational purposes, perhaps by simplifying decision strategies, enhancing accountability, or simply making more defensible decisions. While books such as Mark Pastin's *The Hard Problems of Management: Gaining the Ethics Edge* (1986) seem to imply that we should be ethical because it gives us a competitive advantage, this argument is a dangerous one to pursue because implicit in such a defense of ethical action is that if being ethical does *not* offer a competitive advantage, then one has no justification for doing the right thing. Nevertheless, we might wish to show how ethical behavior can lead to organization improvements in other ways, not as the basic justification for being ethical, but because it is one more way to enlist support for organizational reform. However, such a justification must be clearly subordinate to other justifications for being ethical.

Keeping these objectives in mind, it is vital that we determine precisely what the appropriate changes should be. There have been suggestions from a variety of sources which will be presented and discussed here. How these would apply to public organizations and whether they might be successful in bringing about a more ethical public administration will also be a part of the discussion.

In broad terms, the areas of possible organizational reform could be categorized as: developing an organizational conscience; altering organizational division of task; protecting the ethical individual who violates organizational policies and procedures; and raising the level of ethical discussion as a part of organizational practice. These are broad categories but will be useful in seeing the types of changes possible in organizations and to see what these could contribute to the development of a more ethical public administration. Each will be dealt with in a separate section.

### Developing an Organizational Conscience

There is a fundamental debate in philosophical circles regarding ethics and organizations. That debate centers around whether an *organization* can be considered to have acted in an ethical or unethical manner, or alternatively, if those designations are reserved only for individuals. In other words, if the outcomes of activities within an organization would be considered immoral, can it be said that the organization (as opposed to the individuals within it) is an immoral one, or that the organization acted unethically. In part there is no answer to this question and philosophers will debate it for centuries to come, but it does have some relevance to this discussion and therefore needs to be addressed.

If the activities within an organization result in outcomes that are considered immoral, then there must be some mechanism for attributing responsibility for the actions in order that accountability mechanisms can operate. Some have argued that without accountability, organizations will soon be out of control and unmanageable (Rosen, 1982; Davis, 1969). But when the action results from interrelated organizational activities, attempting to identify who or what is responsible for the action in question will almost surely lead to the conclusion that no individual was actually responsible for the act or the outcomes. Almost always there will be a predecessor or some other individual or group who was just as responsible for what occurred as the individual in question. This is an inevitable problem since others are involved whenever something occurs as a result of organizational activity. The discrete actions of individuals, then, can rarely be judged as harshly as the outcomes would warrant.

Organizations are designed to do more than any of the individuals involved could do separately. Just as an individual would have great difficulty designing and building an entire automobile comparable to what can be done by organizational members acting in unison, so too would an individual have great difficulty in designing and carrying out moral wrongs (or positive moral actions) of the magnitude that can be achieved through organizations. Each individual could be held responsible for the discrete acts taken part in, but the weight of those individual acts will not add up to the overall weight of the wrong (or good) done.

Another method of passing judgment and assuring accountability for organizational outcomes would be to say that the top level administrator should be held morally responsible for all outcomes of the organization. While this may serve the purpose of providing a target for exacting moral revenge after an immoral outcome, it will probably only be misplaced revenge and not moral righteousness. The top administrator, as seen in Kaufman's (1981) study of federal bureau chiefs, rarely has the kind of impact that one would expect in smaller, less complex situations, and therefore cannot reasonably be held morally accountable for all organizational outcomes. At the very least, it would be an insufficient action since it leaves many other wrongdoers unaccountable.

Thus, individual accountability seems an inadequate remedy or preventative for immoral actions, especially in the context of organizational rationality in which individuals frequently assume that someone else will find, resolve, or take responsibility for the problem in question. We can see that placing moral responsbility for organizational outcomes is extremely difficult but nevertheless very important.

The other approach might be to find a way to hold the organization itself accountable for the wrongdoing, but what sense does it make to hold an organization responsible and accountable when the organization is only the structure, rules, and patterns within which individuals operate? This is the basic dilemma discussed by philosophers and faced by a society so strongly influenced by organizations.

Without attempting to resolve the dilemma posed, a way around this can be suggested. It is a natural reaction to an immoral act caused through organizational activity, to condemn the organization as well as to try to find individuals to hold responsible. As a matter of course we do both, whether or not either makes sense given the situation. Given this human response, it would be well to try to hold the organization accountable in ways separate from the individual members. This has been addressed in the legal world by making a corporation a legal person, but morally the problem might not be so easily addressed. One example of it being done might be the practice of the American Association of University Professors (AAUP) to blacklist universities that have violated professors' academic freedom.

There is a positive side to this as well, one which makes an effort to prevent moral wrongdoing rather than redressing it after the fact. Goodpaster and Matthews (1982) have argued that external controls on organizations, and holding individuals accountable for their actions are inadequate for ensuring moral action on the part of organizations. Instead, they suggest that the organization be considered a morally accountable "person" and that efforts be made to develop a conscience within the organization.

If we can say that persons act responsibly only if they gather information about the impact of their actions on others and use it in making decisions, we can reasonably do the same for organizations. Our proposed frame of reference for thinking about and implementing corporate responsibility aims at spelling out the processes associated with the moral responsibility of individuals and projecting them to the level of organizations. (Goodpaster and Matthews, 1982:135)

They go on to argue that some organizations have in fact "built features into their management incentive systems, board structures, internal control systems, and research agendas that in a person we would call self-control, integrity, and conscientiousness" (Goodpaster and Matthews, 1982:135). They provide an excellent defense for attempting to attribute the role of the conscience to the organization, though recognizing that the implications might be disturbing. It is disturbing if viewed as a *substitute* for, rather than a supplement to, individual consciences, especially since it appears that the existing mechanisms for assuring ethical action in organizations are inadequate to the task. There is a risk that this might be viewed as substituting a faulty mechanism of control, for the proven method of individual conscience and self-control.

The primary criticism of using the "organizational conscience" as an ethical reform measure is that it remains *organizational*, and the focus can never be on what the individual or society would consider to be morally right. In other words, because of the nature of organizations (which are a means established to meet some other end) instrumental rationality is a predominant characteristic. The challenge of ethics in organizations is to integrate the morality of the core values of society with the necessity of operating in a functionally rational way, and committees created by organizations might not be sufficiently separate from the logic of instrumental rationality to adequately address broader social concerns. Case 5.B shows the dilemmas of such a situation.

### Case 5.B

In some locations there are insufficient numbers of kidney dialysis machines to meet the needs of clients of public hospitals. In addition, there is always a scarcity of organs available for kidney transplants. These factors necessitate deciding on the order of priority for patients in need of these services. Physicians making independent decisions are unable to distribute the scarce resources in a manner which on the whole is fair, just, and reasonable. Consequently, hospitals are moved to establish committees and charge them with devising plans and making decisions for the distribution of these resources.

In one hospital the committee developed a series of guidelines or rules to follow in allocating the scarce kidneys and dialysis machines. One guideline was the length of time the patient had lived in the county, another was the contribution the patient had made to the community. In another hospital it was decided that less than optimal kidneys would be sold to those best able to pay, reportedly these were most often wealthy individuals from oil rich countries.

When one is making decisions about the life and death of individuals who will not survive if not provided with the necessary transplant or treatment, where one has lived or how much money one has, is of little moral relevance and would probably not be the basis on which an individual health care professional would want to make the decision. However, those considerations are very significant to an organization which is created to serve a particular location, and which must cover its costs.

In trying to establish a conscience within, or through, organizational structures it remains very difficult for the individuals involved to avoid having the decision process dominated by the instrumental rationality of the organization. The decisions made by such organizational committees too easily become depersonalized, dehumanized, and made on the narrow basis of instrumental rationality to the exclusion of individual moral judgment. In part this happens because the committee is physically and emotionally isolated from the individuals affected by the decisions, which would not be the case for doctors who previously made the decisions. Such isolation from those affected by one's decisions can reduce one's sense of the moral magnitude of the decisions being made. On the other hand, the committee might be able to make decisions and establish guidelines in an objective manner which could contribute positively to the overall success of the kidney treatment center. The key issue is not that organizational considerations of costs and location served are irrelevant, but that those must not be the only bases on which life and death decisions are made.

Thus, efforts to reform organizations by creating surrogate consciences, such as the committee described above or the "ethics committees" of other organizations, hold significant promise but must be pursued much more cautiously than other types of reforms. The "organizational conscience" in whatever form it takes is very susceptible to being dominated by instrumental rationality to the exclusion of moral reasoning, and it also contributes to the impression that "someone else" is responsible for the morality of actions carried out in organizations.

The process of developing an organizational conscience, though, can serve some useful purposes in a broad sense. Such efforts will implicitly express organizational support for high ethical standards among members of the organization. Of course, this will happen only if the organizational efforts do not supplant the efforts of the individuals. The process also provides a means by which individuals can raise moral and ethical questions with their colleagues in an organizationally approved manner. The notion that one needs organizational approval to raise moral and ethical issues is quite problematic because one of the primary objectives of developing ethical consciousness on the part of administrators is to help them raise ethical questions in spite of organizational or other resistance. But, if one accepts the argument that individuals tend to adopt patterns of behavior which are approved as acceptable within the organization, then this approach to ethical reform must not be overlooked as a useful supplement to raised individual consciousness.

Other reforms also need to be undertaken in order to enhance the opportunities for the individual conscience to operate within the organizational framework. One such reform is altering the division of tasks and authority within the organization.

## Altering Divisions of Task and Authority

One of the primary reasons that it is difficult to practice ethical behavior within organizations is the division of task, which fractionates jobs to such a large extent. With no one responsible for the entire task, it is difficult to find someone with both the information and authority to resolve the ethical problems that will be encountered. One solution to the problem, then, would be to divide work within an organization in a more holistic manner.

By assigning a problem or a large task to an individual or to a small group, it will contribute to a larger frame of reference and improve the ability of individuals to identify ethical issues and make decisions about those issues. Having responsibility for a whole task, or for the resolution of a problem, gives the individual involved a better frame of reference while at the same time fixing greater responsibility on the individual for the outcomes. This greater sense of responsibility will affect both the technical aspects of a job, perhaps leading to more creativity and better solutions, and the ethical dimensions of the job, perhaps leading to more ethically defensible solutions.

A major problem with redesigning work is the potential loss of efficiency. Jobs were divided and simplified in order to achieve greater efficiency, and any approach to improving the ethical actions of individuals which compromises efficiency significantly is unlikely to succeed in practice. But restructuring work does not necessarily decrease efficiency. In fact, many organizations have found that work which has become too simplified and too removed from a vision of the whole task and its relationship to other tasks, soon becomes boring and unsatisfying work, with the quality of the product or service suffering.

One of the most frequently suggested methods of improving productivity and efficiency in such cases involves restructuring and redesigning work. The various approaches to redesign share two common objectives: developing a greater sense of responsibility within the individual for the product or service being produced, and assigning work in such a way that the employee can relate individual efforts to the broader vision of organizational purposes and to the finished product.

The same principles for redesigning work for greater productivity can be applied to redesigning work for improved ethical standards and outcomes. The latter will not occur simply because the work has been redesigned; therefore it must be accompanied by a development of the ethical consciousness of the individuals as well.

In addition to redesigning tasks in order to develop a more

holistic approach to work, there must be more decentralization of authority to accompany the redesign. Delegating authority as well as responsibility for a task to the lowest possible level of the organization enhances the outcomes in terms of effectiveness as well as in terms of the ethics of those outcomes. When the organizational member who must actually perform a task has the authority to make decisions about how and when that task is done, it can significantly increase the effectiveness with which the task is carried out. One need only refer to the numerous examples of employees who have offered suggestions saving the organization thousands of dollars each year or significantly improving the service or product, but did so only when explicitly asked for their suggestions, rather than twenty years earlier when the idea came to them. Had those employees been given the authority to make those decisions or felt enough efficacy to make the suggestion to someone with authority, those improvements would have been achieved much sooner.

The practice of delegating authority and responsibility to the lowest reasonable level is just as relevant for developing ethical capacities as it is for developing capacity for productivity, quality or excellence. The person performing the task is in an ideal position to assess the outcomes of the action in terms of human impact and in consideration of core social values which are enhanced or not enhanced by the action. Having the authority to make decisions related to the task one is assigned enhances individual responsibility, and experience using that authority will enhance ethical deliberation capabilities.

Case 5.B illustrates that point. When removed from the human effects of their decisions, the committee tended to also be removed from the moral significance of those decisions, and began to rely exclusively on instrumental rationality in developing the guidelines. Those who cannot remove themselves from the human impact of their decisions because they experience the human impact while implementing the policy, are more likely to apply moral standards in their decision making because their sense of morality will be triggered in a way that isn't possible when decisions are made in isolation of the decision's impact.

One problem with delegating responsibility and authority to

lower levels of the hierarchy is that all of the relevant values and objectives might not be taken into consideration. Policies, implementing activities, and outcomes must be consistent with political and organizational needs as well as core social values and human consideration. There is no question that delegation of authority and responsibility must be accompanied by some measure of control over the actions and decisions of members of the organization. However, measures to enhance account-ability for *outcomes* could replace some of the centralization of authority which is the control method used most often in the past. In addition, some of the suggestions made by Davis (1969) and others about structuring the discretionary power of admin-istrators could be applied in the organizational process.

Given the fact that organizational objectives such as survival, budget enhancement, as well as efficiency and effectiveness are so engrained in organizational culture and standard operating procedures, it is unlikely that consideration of the moral rami-fications of policies will completely overshadow these objec-tives. And political objectives can be assured of consideration through the dual mechanisms of the boundaries set by the leg-islative mandate, and the oversight mechanisms of both the legislative and executive branches of government.

In spite of these assurances that there will be appropriate checks on discretion, it must be recognized that when organi-zational members are allowed and encouraged to make discre-tionary judgments in their work, those judgments will some-times result in embarrassment or harm to the organization, and at other times will not be good judgments. Therefore, account-ability mechanisms (discussed in Chapter 4) must operate in order to prevent unsound decision making from detracting from the efforts of the organization. At other times, the judgments might be quite sound but nevertheless result in embarrassment or harm to the organization, such as cases in which unreason-able or ineffective policies are openly criticized by a member of the organization. In order that the individual be protected from retribution when the discretionary decisions are sound ones but embarrassing for the organization, there must be some estab-lished method of assuring that the individual will be protected.

## Protecting the Individual

A frequently expressed concern is that when individuals within organizations do take it upon themselves to point out what they believe to be unethical or otherwise inappropriate practices (i.e., blow the whistle), their efforts often meet a great deal of resistance from others in the organization. Superiors see it as an affront to their authority, pathological behavior, or as a challenge to the organizational imperative which they find it useful to protect. Peers and subordinates are also often reluctant to express support, either because of fear for the future of the organization, or through fear for their own jobs. The whistle-blower is frequently (though not always) going beyond the limits of the authority and responsibility of his or her organizational position in raising the issue, or in some other way is violating the norms of the organization. This often leads to punishment, isolation, or other forms of retribution. This fact points to some very difficult issues to deal with in organizations.

"Blowing the whistle" in an organization involves finding serious fault with a decision or action, so even when the judgment is correct and appropriate, someone in the organization probably has a vested interest in seeing that the information is not uncovered. Others who have an interest in covering up the supposed wrongdoing (perhaps by discrediting the whistle-blower) might do so in order to protect the reputation of the organization, the practice which has become standard procedure in the organization, or to protect themselves from the embarrassment of not having made the same judgment earlier. Those at the top of the hierarchy might wish to protect the organization from bad press, or protect the investment of time, money, and other resources that have already been made. Such an effort to protect the organization even at the expense of hurting others is clearly a case of organizational rationality overcoming individual rationality and individual ethics.

In spite of recent publicity and even legislation designed to assure protection for those who dissent (e.g., the Merit System Protection Board), whistle-blowers often find little or no support and may in fact find that they have no job or prospects for jobs in the future because they attempted to do what they considered ethically right. This phenomenon has precipitated a new and growing body of literature dealing with whistle-blowing. In an overview of that literature, James S. Bowman (1983b) found there are two broad substantive issues which must be addressed by public administration: "First is bureaucratic responsibility and accountability. . . . Ways need to be found to introduce democratic rights into agencies. . . . Secondly, due process procedures are necessary to protect employee-critics in order to guarantee responsibility and accountability" (Bowman, 1983b:271). This is an indication that unless such hindrances to ethical action are addressed in organizations, administrative ethics reform will not result in more ethical practice.

Protection of the individual's rights and obligation to make ethical judgments within the organization can take a variety of forms. The step which has been taken most often of late is to develop due process procedures to provide some protection and recourse to those individuals who perceive that they have been treated unfairly as a result of their whistle-blowing. This type of organizational response has two positive aspects: first, it indicates to employees that the organization is supportive of efforts to enhance the ethical dimensions of the organization; and second, it provides recourse for those who have encountered negative responses to their efforts to do the first.

While developing methods of organizational due process is a necessary step which almost any organization can undertake, it will not be *sufficient* to address the large problem of administrative ethics for two reasons. First, it in no way assures change in the unethical activity. In other words, due process may help protect an individual employee, but it does not help accomplish the ends sought by the whistle-blower. Second, due process procedures in an organization cannot assure that the whistle-blower will not encounter harassment or maltreatment by superiors and peers. It can provide recourse if harassment or other forms of punishment occur, but it cannot prevent the harassment except in the most indirect of ways. Many whistle-blowers report that they have experienced a great deal of personal and professional loss as a result of their attempts to be ethical, and failure to establish reforms which help prevent such loss will serve as a deterrence to future whistle-blowers.

A second method of dealing with the problem within the organization is to create an office or position through which whistle-blowers could anonymously report the observed unethical behaviors or policies. The office, rather than the individual, would then pursue the investigation. This is the rationale behind the Special Counsel's Office, which was created for the federal Civil Service. Thus, the whistle-blower need not fear personal retribution for reporting the wrongdoing, and there is an outside party charged with investigating the incident.

This in some ways resolves the problems associated with only assuring due process for the individual but it creates others. For example, an anonymous tip from an employee can lead to the investigation of an incident, but it cannot lead to a dialogue between the accuser and the accused. Such dialogue is valuable in preventing unfounded accusations, but more importantly it contributes to the overall development of an ethical public administration. Louis Gawthrop (1984) emphasizes this point in *Public Sector Management, Systems, and Ethics*:

The institutionalization of critical operational evaluation involves more than the establishment of an inspector general's office or an ombudsman's office. It means developing an institutional environment wherein public managers are expected to think independently, critically, and constructively. (Gawthrop, 1984:6)

If public administration ethics is to be seriously pursued, it is necessary for members of public organizations to more actively engage in discussion and debate about the ethical implications of policies, procedures, activities and other aspects of organizational life. Only by encouraging this discourse can we expect that the level of discussion and behavior would move to a higher plane.

In addition, reporting wrongdoing to another office leads to the types of bureaucratic problems associated with all organizations. The case load can become too heavy, the backlog too great, and the outlook of the employees jaded. That will contribute little to improving the overall level of ethical behavior.

Nevertheless, the special office could make a positive contribution if not seen as the only way to handle encounters with wrongdoing.

Another suggestion for protecting the individual whistle-blower is through what Jaques (1976) calls "constitutional bureaucracy." Organizations of this sort clearly define authority at all levels and elected employee representatives participate in establishing policies. Consultation, recognition of diverse interests, and negotiation are consistently a part of the normal operation of a constitutional bureaucracy, building in protections for individuals who challenge current practices (Cooper, 1982:132).

Gawthrop also suggest reforms which involve "the development of a new organizational design to deal effectively with the complexities of the public policy process and the increasing complexities of organizational environments" (Gawthrop, 1984:119). Like Jaques, these design changes are intended to result in more positive experiences for the organizational member, but also to produce better public policy outcomes.

Designing organizations in these ways might help alleviate many problems, but the lack of ready examples of such designs attests to the difficulty of implementing the changes. It would be naive to suggest that reforms of this nature would be received with universal enthusiasm. The consequences of reform are not only greater opportunities for ethical deliberation, but also a related increase in power and authority for subordinates. Those changes are likely to run counter to the organizational imperative, and the desire of the superiors to maintain their power base.

But, the benefits of protecting individuals who blow the whistle, and of considering organizational design changes, extend beyond the improvement of ethical deliberation. It also improves accountability, responsiveness, and in most cases will also improve the policy outcomes. These outcomes would be enhanced even further if accompanied by efforts to enhance the level of ethical deliberation and discussion among organizational members, the last organizational response which will be discussed.

## Enhancing Ethical Discourse

Boling and Dempsey (1981) suggested that one organizational response to unethical organizational behavior is "normative enrichment." By this they mean "an evaluation of overall organizational conduct, clarification of rules, and normative training for organization members" (Boling and Dempsey, 1981:17). The normative enrichment puts members into a psychological environment in which they can give their attention to the premises of decision making in their organization—the rules, regulations, and standards of behavior which are expected of organizational members. Boling and Dempsey suggest that the organization must "adopt a definite normative stance toward its environment," establish a "normative profile of the organization," and finally that "organizational rules for conduct should be made specific and very public" (Boling and Dempsey, 1981:17). This last suggestion is similar to the Davis (1969) suggestion that discretion be structured by making standards which inform discretionary decisions, both public and formal.

Probably the most important aspect of this suggestion of normative enrichment is that it provides an *opportunity* to discover, discuss, and make normative judgments about the decision premises present in any organization. An environment that not only provides an opportunity for discussion, but encourages such efforts can result in several positive outcomes. First, there will be a much-needed dialogue about ethical issues, which can help individuals to make judgments in a responsible way, considering not only their personal views but also those of other individuals as well as the views and needs of the organization. It is a highly personalized approach which could yield valuable breakthroughs in the ethical dimensions of a particular organization. A feeling of shared concern about the ethical dilemmas of a particular profession or type of endeavor would be quite beneficial in terms of helping individuals develop their own sense of moral concerns and convictions, as well as a recognition of the duties and obligations of others, which they must make decisions in accord with. However, it is important that the "ethical forums" be conducted in a way that encourages the integration of these ethical concerns into the daily activities of the administrator so that ethics does not become something considered in isolation of day-to-day decision making.

Second, this open discourse might provide the opportunity to engage in direct and open discussion about specific incidents. Whether this is the appropriate forum for discussions between accuser and accused will depend on the particular way this forum is structured. It is important not to undercut the primary purpose (to enhance ethical discourse) by making participants fearful of accusations. But if such a trade-off is not implied, then this might be an appropriate time and place for addressing specific incidents.

A third positive outcome might be that ethical discourse could contribute to the development of creative alternatives to organizational, individual, or policy difficulties. Problems or difficult situations can be exposed to discourse among a variety of people in a forum outside of the usual decision-making setting, with new perspectives and the freedom to look at the problem in a different light. Unencumbered by the limitations usually perceived, the solutions could well be more creative, more inclusive, and indeed better in ways other than just being more ethically sound.

A danger is that there would be a tendency to institutionalize reform, which might lead to cooptation by the power structure in the organization. If the "normative discourse" becomes a forum for rationalizing and defending existing organizational processes and procedures, then it has served only to effectively counter the voice of dissent within the organization. Thus, institutionalizing this type of discourse requires a commitment to make appropriate changes, and a commitment to some set of goals, values, or purposes (e.g., professional ethics) which will counter the tendency to rationalize existing organizational practice.

It would be all too easy for the discussions in these forums to be restricted to organizationally approved methods and organizationally approved concerns. Such limitations would violate the objectives of engaging in normative discourse. Boling and Dempsey (1981) suggest that it might be possible to expand the perspective of the discussions by emphasizing professional norms, codes of ethics, or other professional concerns in order to avoid total domination by the perspective of the home organization. This approach of extending one's perspective beyond the immediate organization holds significant promise for public organizations, but has two potential limitations.

The "profession" of public administration is not clearly defined and might not be the same profession for all those involved in normative discourse—social workers, health professionals, accountants, and engineers might reasonably turn to those professions in seeking ethical guidance or a broader perspective. For the field of public administration this means that the perspectives brought into the normative discourse might well be very diverse which would necessitate a considerable effort, in the beginning, to develop a common language and shared understanding of the issues. Perhaps of greater concern is that with loyalties to differing professional organizations it might be difficult for public employees to maintain an ongoing awareness of the *public* nature of their work which might differ significantly from their private sector counterparts in those professional organizations. In other words, the diverse views might contribute to lively debate but they won't necessarily share a common foundation in the concern for the public interest.

This requires that public administration develop more fully the ethical foundation of its own profession, so that all the professionals within public administration could have one common foundation. One approach to this might be to suggest that the common foundation for public administration ethics rests on the fundamental moral order of the society, and that the values of the various professions would rarely come into legitimate conflict with those moral principles. Developing this common foundation into a coherent form will be a long and difficult task, but the basic concept of the fundamental moral order could serve as a starting point for the discussion of various professions seeking agreement on ethical practice.

The second limitation associated with an organization's efforts to enhance ethical discourse is that the broadening of perspective within the organization must be legitimized and encouraged even with full recognition that such a perspective will sometimes constitute a challenge to the primary organizational objectives of efficiency and effectiveness. Implicit in this kind of reform effort is the demand that moral considerations receive adequate attention in the decision-making process within the organization, and that these considerations not be routinely ignored in favor of the expediency of meeting the instrumental objectives of the organization.

It is difficult to imagine that the organizational imperative described by Scott and Hart would permit such a challenge. Perhaps it can be argued, though, that the broadening of perspective in public organizations is demanded by the public when it demands responsiveness and responsibility of public administrators as well as efficiency and effectiveness. In addition, the broader perspective achieved by looking beyond the needs of the organization might yield ideas and innovations which actually contribute to the effective functioning of the organization.

One caution should be emphasized: simply adopting a wider perspective and approving points of view broader than the parochial interests of the organization in no way guarantees that the ethical tenor will be improved. A broadened perspective helps to avoid some pervasive problems associated with "organizational blinders" but the perspective which is adopted must still be founded on the clear and explicit articulation of the values to be pursued in public organizations. Some of those values might be unique to public administrators, such as pursuit of the public interest or protection of "regime values," but other values to be articulated will be an outgrowth of our shared sense of the moral order.

## ORGANIZATIONAL REFORM: THE CASE FOR CHANGE

Organizational reform could be among the most significant actions taken to improve the ethical tenor of public administration. At the same time it will probably be the area of greatest challenge since the existing norms and structures which are so functional in serving organizational purposes are also one source that inhibits ethical deliberation. Organizational change will be fundamental to any significant advances in administrative ethics, but will be very difficult to bring about. The difficulties are not likely to arise because public employees as moral individuals resist those changes, but instead because persons in organizational roles will resist those changes in an effort to do what they think is best for the organization—this might be described as the "organizational imperative" in action.

Few people consider themselves unethical, but most express much less confidence in the ethics of their colleagues. One of the key arguments for the centralization of authority is the need to control others in order to prevent unethical or irresponsible behavior. A renewed confidence in the ethics of one's peers and subordinates will be necessary to bring about the loosening of controls which will allow individuals to make decisions about ethics and their work, whatever their level in the organization. The renewed confidence will only come about if there is evidence to suggest that one's co-workers are able to make moral judgments with which one would usually agree. One way to bring about that realization is to increase the ethical training of all public administrators (through the standard educational curriculum or in-service training), and another way is to foster ethical discussions within organizations, which should provide ample evidence that most people share common ethical standards and wish to apply those standards to their work as well as to their personal lives.

What are the incentives for making significant organizational changes? Several were mentioned in the discussion of proposed reform measures. Some of the reform measures could actually contribute to increased effectiveness and creativity within the organization by broadening the perspectives of those engaged in problem solving and decision making. In addition, there is a clear message that society demands a more ethically responsible public sector just as there has been considerable social pressure on the private sector so be more "socially conscious."

Public organizations need to be responsive to these social demands and expectations, and will have to devise ways of responding just as businesses have been attempting to do (however imperfectly). If we hope to avoid the often-used corporate strategy of substituting elaborate public relations campaigns for substantive changes in administrative and organizational practice, public administration will need to make considerable efforts to devise, encourage, and implement better alternatives.

# 6

# ETHICS IN PRACTICE: AN APPLICATION

The objective of this book has been to develop an approach to public administration ethics that is both theoretically sound and practical. The discussion has focused on how administrators should act—personally, professionally, and as members of organizations. Suggestions have been made regarding how to influence individuals to act in a more ethical manner, and influence organizations to accommodate and encourage such ethical action. Now we must determine whether the framework and suggestions developed in previous chapters can be useful in guiding administrative action. In this chapter, a case prepared by John Nalbandian of the University of Kansas will be presented and the model will be applied in an analysis of the case. By applying the model to a specific administrative case we will be able to determine if it will be tenable in practice, and whether it has a sufficiently strong theoretical base to accommodate the complexities of administrative practice.

## A CASE STUDY (BY JOHN NALBANDIAN)

A simple problem seemed to be developing into one with troubling dimensions. The Secretary of the State Department of Social Welfare, an old pro, had submitted the agency's budget for next year to the Governor's office for review and inclusion in the Governor's submission to the legislature. The Governor's office had assigned a relatively inexperienced analyst to review the agency's budget and he passed it along with few questions, paying more attention to other budget requests he had inferred from his conversations with legislators would be more controversial.

The legislature, looking for ways to trim the budget, sharply scrutinized the Governor's budget. Their projections of available revenue compared very unfavorably with the Governor's, and they were in a feisty mood.

The legislative review committee picked up on what the Secretary at first believed was an inconsequential matter: caseload for income maintenance workers. During each of the previous two years, caseloads had increased to meet budget cutbacks, and employee morale had suffered. The Governor's revenue projection would permit the Department of Welfare to reinstate the original work standard, while the legislature's projection would increase the caseload standard even over the most recent year's standard. In fact, the legislative committee focused on this particular issue even though by all conventions caseload standards should have been considered an administrative matter.

The out-party legislators on the budget review committee began to make an issue out of the Governor's budget, particularly the Welfare Department's proposed appropriation, and not surprisingly linked the proposed appropriation to increasing the welfare caseloads. While this seemed a ridiculous link and a frivolous matter, it nonetheless put the Governor in a very uncomfortable spot, to say the least; and it put the Secretary on the hot seat.

The simple solution would have been to hold the old line on caseload and live with the morale problem. But, as soon as the

issue reached the press, the Welfare Mothers' Association re-
acted with a vehement attack on the out-party legislative leadership, and to cover all bases they organized a one day sit-in
at the busiest local welfare office. To complicate matters, a few
of the income maintenance workers in that office let it be known
that their sympathies went to the welfare mothers. This pro-
nouncement outraged the out-party leadership and sealed the
fate on the caseload issue. Under no circumstances would the
welfare budget be appropriated as proposed, no reduction in
the caseload standard could be expected, and minimum eligibility requirements would be affected.

The Secretary's sympathies for several years had aligned her
not only with her employees, but with the clients as well. In
fact, last year she had felt the last straw had been drawn on
the caseload issue and minimum eligibility requirement, and
the only light in the whole situation was the expectation that
the budget would be increased this year with reductions in
caseload and easing of income maintenance income minimums.

The Governor called the Secretary and after hearing again
her dismay said, "Whatever you decide to do, I'll back you."
The Secretary was prepared to resign on moral grounds. The
clients would not be served by the budget reduction, and the
employees deserved better. In addition, she had heard that the
welfare mothers would not take a cutback in benefits lightly
and that there were rumblings of a movement to unionize the
income maintenance workers. She thought to herself, "Who
needs this?"

When indications of her intentions entered the rumor mill,
life's pace increased dramatically. Figuratively, all business of
the agency ceased while the Secretary's future was speculated
upon. The next day, the Secretary's division directors requested an appointment with the Secretary, and all but one
urged her to stay, arguing that the agency had more constituents than welfare mothers, and that with the Secretary's leadership all clients of the agency except the welfare mothers had
benefited and these gains surely would be jeopardized with the
Secretary's resignation. The lone dissenter was responsible for
the Income Maintenance program. That afternoon, representa-

tives of the Association for the Humane Treatment of Mentally Retarded Children met with the Secretary and they also urged her to remain, pointing to a legislative program for these children that was just half-way complete and whose successful enactment everyone acknowledged would depend on the Secretary's leadership.

Meanwhile, the Governor's office was getting itchy with all the publicity since it seemed the out-party, in defense, was going after the Governor's budget with vengeance commensurate with publicity about the Secretary's future. The Secretary was not immune to the pressure on the Governor and realized that her resignation might well prove the best course of action if only on political grounds.

That night the Secretary received a call from Wanda Flemming, a branch chief in the Department of Corrections. In a hesitant way Wanda let the Secretary know that as the only female in the Governor's cabinet, she was held in high esteem by other women and was a role model for many. The Secretary was touched by the call, and then sat down to consider her options, none of which she would wish on her worst enemy.

She thought she couldn't live with the inevitable budget cut, with its effect on the welfare mothers and income maintenance workers, but in her heart she knew that other constituents depended on her. There were a lot of other factors as well that complicated the situation. But what really disturbed her was the thought that originally she felt compelled by a moral concern to take a stand against the legislature's action. Now with all the countervailing influences she was not only unsure about a course of action, she was convinced that she was dealing with a political issue, not an ethical one.

## ANALYSIS

The Secretary in this case faces competing sets of obligations and responsibilities, each with some moral relevance—in other words, an ethical dilemma. Obligations to clients and employees conflict with obligations to the Governor and to the legislature. Obligations to one set of clients conflict with obligations to other clients. There are political, moral, and professional dimensions to the situation, all of which demand consideration by the Secretary but which incline her toward different decisions.

Because the situation occurs in a politically volatile context, the Secretary has come to doubt that she is dealing with an ethical dilemma, and to wonder if instead she should treat it as a political issue. One might surmise that this response is a natural one when the ethical dilemma poses such a difficult choice for an administrator, while the political choice seems more obvious. The ethical framework developed earlier, however, suggests that the administrator is obligated to consider the ethical dimensions of her actions even though the political dimensions seem compelling.

In order to make an ethical decision in this case, the Secretary must first acknowledge and assess her full range of obligations and responsibilities as an individual and as an administrator. By doing this, she will be in a position to make reasoned choices among alternative courses of action, taking into consideration the ethical implications of the choices. Second, the Secretary must take personal responsibility for making the decision in an ethical manner. This implies that she must not make a decision based solely on the wishes, expectations, or demands of others involved in the case. Her own conscience must be her guide in the final decision. Third, in order to make an ethical decision she must critically analyze the underlying assumptions of each course of action in order that she better understand the value choices being made. Finally, she must apply some decision standards or principles, and reach a decision.

The first two steps mentioned (assessing obligations and responsibilities, and taking personal responsibility for the decision) require an exploration of the social, organizational, and professional roles and expectations of the administrator. The next section addresses those issues. The last two steps require an assessment of the options available to the Secretary, and the application of ethical standards. The ''Recommendations'' section will outline the choices to be made, analyze those choices, and suggest ethical principles which should guide the decisions to be made.

**The Role of the Public Administrator:**
**Social, Organizational, and Professional**

In this case, the Secretary of the Department of Social Welfare appears to be cognizant of the full range of roles and expectations placed upon her and is duly considering them in
making a decision. The roles and expectations will be outlined
briefly as the framework for ethical administration is applied.

The Secretary encounters this situation because of the actions
of the legislature, and therefore we will first examine the role
of the administrator in that context. The federal civil service
reform measures taken early in this century represented an effort to make public administration less political, more effective,
and more accountable. At first, this was interpreted as requiring a role for administrators based on a politics/administration
dichotomy:

This tradition, in short, developed two conceptual yardsticks: (1) politics sets the task for administration, but administration lies outside
the proper sphere of politics and, as such, (2) administration can be
transformed into a science. (Rabin and Bowman, 1984:4–5)

More recently that interpretation has undergone extensive
revision, and public administration is viewed not only as a science (though an imperfect one) but also as a political and value-
laden activity. A key issue, though, is how much of a political,
advocacy, or policy-making role the administrator should play
in addition to the role of administering the policies of others.
"The proper place for public administration along a politics-
administration continuum, therefore, has been a source of continuing controversy. Given the nature of the political system,
this debate probably never can be resolved fully" (Rabin and
Bowman, 1984:8). Administrators such as the Secretary in the
case being analyzed must make decisions without benefit of
the resolution of the ongoing debate.

For the Secretary, administering the policies made in the political realm presents serious problems. Those policies, she believes, will in some sense bring harm to clients and employees,
and the Secretary sees this as undue and unfair harm. Were a

strict politics/administration dichotomy generally accepted, the Secretary would have little difficulty justifying to herself and to others the choice to yield to the legislative decision. But, the Secretary and many other relevant actors (employees and client groups, for example) view the obligations of the administrator as more than the implementation arm of the political body, and such a justification would not be accepted.

The administrator is expected, by herself and others, to play an advocacy role in the policy-making process, in order to bring about political and bureaucratic actions addressing the needs of clients and employees. If the Secretary had instead claimed as her role the administration of whatever policies are made by the legislature, she would have violated the role expectations society has developed for public administrators, and she would have violated professional and ethical norms regarding the administrative role.

Another ambiguous dimension of the administrator's role as a part of the politics/administration continuum has to do with the division of authority between the administrative and political bodies. This dimension involves determining which decisions should reasonably reside within the administrative function rather than being subject to political debate. In this case, that dimension is represented by the issue of determining caseload for income maintenance workers. This decision is "policy making" in the sense that it influences the service that clients can expect to receive from their case worker, and in the sense that it influences the allocation of public funds. But, it would normally be considered a part of the administrative function in that it involves the implementation of a policy and not the substance of a policy. Because the division of task and authority between the bureaucracy and the legislature is not clearly defined, a situation arises in which the legislature can, and does, make a decision about the caseload even though ill-equipped to make that decision. The administrator, who was well-equipped to make the decision, seems not to have sufficient definition of administrative authority to compel the legislature to abandon the course of action.

This is a clear example of the problems that organizational task and authority structures can present to public administrators. Even in those areas which would normally be considered their responsibility, administrators are subject to the review and authority of political bodies. Those political bodies can and do make decisions the administrator will be expected to implement, and which the administrator might have great difficulty in supporting. This is particularly troublesome because as Davis argued, "administrators must share the responsibility for producing legislation that is sound, workable, and just . . . " (Davis, 1969:53), yet the administrator has very little leverage for asserting influence on a decision for which she is to share responsibility.

The Secretary is faced with a situation that might have been avoided had the organization and decision-making process been structured according to the guidelines suggested in Chapter 4. Specifically, the authority to determine caseloads for agency employees is appropriately delegated to the administrator of the agency and need not be authority retained by the political body. In this case, the legislature chose to usurp authority of the administrator and made a decision without adequate efforts to gather information and insight about the situation. The resulting decision might be interpreted (and seems to have been interpreted by the Secretary) as unethical or immoral in the sense that it was unfair and unjust treatment of employees.

The structure of decision-making authority in this case can be identified as a contributing factor to the problem, but unfortunately the identification of "cause" does not make a solution any more apparent. The Secretary still must decide how to handle the situation, knowing that the legislators have indeed taken that authority for themselves, and knowing that as a public administrator she is subject to legislative action and responsible to the legislature as well as to the Governor.

The dilemma facing the Secretary does not just involve the issue of caseload, however. The policy regarding the income requirements for the Income Maintenance program also presents an ethical problem for her, but not for the same reasons as the case load issue. The policy regarding income requirements for income maintenance recipients might be argued as appropriately made by the legislature. This policy involves a judgment about the level of need which must be established before public assistance is appropriately given. This is, at least in part, a value judgment of the type that should be an expression of societal values regarding the entitlement of a member of society to public support. It can be argued that those values are best expressed through the public policy-making process as it occurs in the legislative arena.

Thus, while the Secretary of the Department of Social Welfare might believe that the policy decision is unfair to the client group, the *process* for arriving at that decision was probably not unfair and for that reason necessitates special consideration for compliance. This distinction should have some influence on her decision about whether or not to challenge the legislative action, and on what basis to challenge the decision. This distinction also represents a very important responsibility of public administrators: When an administrator disagrees with a policy, it is essential to consider the legitimacy of the decision process as well as the content of the decision when determining what action to take.

Even when the policy-making process appropriately places authority for making a decision with the legislature, the administrator is still expected to play a role in that process. In this case, it is the obligation of the Secretary to play an advocacy role for the clients of her agency during legislative deliberations. She would be expected to do so as a part of her professional and ethical obligations as a public administrator. Deciding not to respond to legislative action on behalf of her clients and employees would be an abdication of her responsibilities.

At the same time, the adminstrator has obligations to other organizational goals beyond the Income Maintenance program. There are obligations to the other client groups who are served by her agency, and (though less directly) broader obligations such as to other programs in the Governor's budget which could be jeopardized by some of her actions. She takes on those broader obligations as a part of her role as one person on the Governor's cabinet, the goals of the Governor's office extend beyond the Department of Social Welfare, and as a part of that team the Secretary must acknowledge her responsibility to the other programs.

One further consideration for the Secretary is the role she plays in the larger social context, beyond the agency, the government, and the immediate needs of client groups. Because she is one of very few women who serve in high-level administrative positions, to some extent her actions will have an influence on other women. That influence comes from the fact that she serves as a role model to some, and the fact that she serves as a "test case" for persons who are considering placing women in high-level administrative positions. Therefore, the impact of her decisions will reach beyond the Department of Social Welfare and into a larger segment of the society. Many people who are in a position of being "the first" or "the only" wish to avoid the label of being a representative of their group and prefer not to have the responsibility of not only their own futures but the futures of others like them. This is a perfectly understandable reluctance, but one cannot ethically choose to avoid such responsibility just because it is uncomfortable. Instead, the Secretary must make a judgment about whether her decision will, in fact, adversely or positively affect the opportunities of other women. If she determines that her actions will have an impact, then those considerations must become a part of the decision-making process.

According to Mertins and Hennigan (1982), as a member of the public administration profession, the Secretary of the Department of Social Welfare is expected to behave in a manner which is characterized by: (1) knowledge of and adherence to the law; (2) performance of tasks in a responsible, knowledgeable, and effective manner; (3) accountability to the public and the organization; and (4) responsiveness to the changing needs of the public.

Given those expectations of the professional, the Secretary in the case would, all else being equal, be obligated to abide by the decision of the legislature once it has become law. As mentioned earlier, this obligation exists because of the legitimacy of the process that brought about the legislative action.

In addition, she has an obligation to perform her job in an effective manner, which might be interpreted as meaning that she must maintain sufficiently good relations with the legislature that her performance and the resources of the agency are not hindered to the point of ineffectiveness. An extension of this reasoning might lead one to argue that the professional obligations to the agency and to client groups require that the Secretary have very good moral reasons for resigning when that resignation will have an impact on the effectiveness of the agency and its ability to meet client needs. In other words, if the Secretary were to resign out of disgust (i.e., "Who needs this?") then she might be ignoring her professional responsibilities.

As a professional public administrator the Secretary will be held accountable to the public, the profession, and the organization for the actions she chooses to take. She will be held accountable by the legislature, the governor, the media, and various client groups including the Welfare Mothers Association and the Association for the Humane Treatment of Mentally Retarded Children. Unfortunately, the different groups are asking for different, and mutually exclusive, actions from the administrator. By way of ordering those responsibilities, the Mertins and Hennigan workbook on professional standards suggests that the "public administrator is answerable first to the public and second to his or her organization" and that such accountability "involves generating and providing credible, accurate information that facilitates evaluations . . . by the public, the employing agency, client groups, and the profession" (Mertins and Hennigan, 1982:6–7). Thus, the Secretary must provide adequate information and justification for her decision to all those affected groups.

Finally, the public administrator as a professional is expected to be responsive to the changing needs of the society, including clients, employees, and the general public. In this case, the general public *might* be best served by a trimmed state budget which would suggest that the legislature's budget-cutting proposals might be in the public interest. In being responsive to the needs of client and employee groups as well as society, the administrator might determine that the public interest would be better served by cuts elsewhere in the state or agency budget. Unfortunately, the legislature controls and seems to have closed that avenue for action.

As a professional, the Secretary has an obligation to have knowledge of, and try to effectively meet, the needs of her client group and her employees. But in this situation, that professional responsibility is in conflict with her obligation to her organizational superior, the Governor. Her obligation to the Governor includes not only doing her job in an effective manner, but doing so in a way that does not endanger other objectives or programs in the Governor's office. In this case, the Secretary rather inadvertently has created problems for the Governor and his budget, and this should be a consideration in her deliberations over which course of action to take.

In addition to the characteristics of professional behavior mentioned above, the administrator is also expected to apply moral standards in administrative action. This expectation is important to mention, because the obligations to clients, employees, the organization, and the profession all set certain standards for administrative behavior, but these must be balanced with the usually implicit expectation that the administrator also act as protector of other social values and standards. A number of relevant moral principles have been suggested in previous chapters, including justice, equity, freedom, and honesty, by which administrators would reasonably be expected to judge their own actions and the actions of others.

The Secretary's decision, then, becomes one in which she must order her priorities regarding moral judgments, in addition to balancing her professional roles and obligations. There are no easy solutions to this case. Some valued outcome will be compromised no matter which choice is made, and some group will suffer undesirable consequences no matter which of the avenues she chooses. She recognizes the relevance of applying ethical standards to administrative decisions in addition to applying professional standards, but that still does not provide a solution to the dilemma. The first two steps have been taken toward making an ethical decision: she has recognized and considered the full range of obligations and responsibilities she must consider, and she has accepted personal responsibility for making the decision. Now she must examine the specific courses of action open to her and make a judgment.

## MAKING ETHICAL DECISIONS ABOUT MORAL DILEMMAS

Having recognized the many responsibilities she must balance, the administrator must determine the courses of action open to her and analyze the assumptions and ethical implications of those options before coming to some decision. The possible actions open to her are presented in Figure 6.1.

Her first step in coming to a decision should be to critically analyze the assumptions and values that guide each of the avenues of action she could take. As discussed in Chapter 2, there are two major frames of reference for thinking about moral issues, a deontological framework and a teleological framework. In the deontological framework of reference, a moral principle can be sufficiently compelling that it would justify a decision regardless of the consequences of that decision. In the teleological frame of reference, no moral principle can provide *a priori* justification for a course of action. The justification only comes in the form of the impact or results of the action. These two frames of reference will be compared and contrasted in the following analysis.

In terms of political expediency the Secretary suggests that it would probably be best to resign in this situation in order to minimize the losses to the agency and to the Governor. Im-

**Figure 6.1**
**Decision Options**

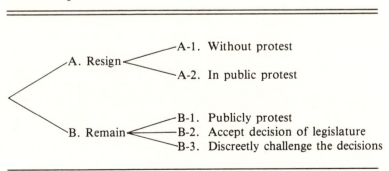

plied in this reasoning is that she would not openly protest the decisions of the legislature because that would continue to embarrass the Governor and jeopardize the budget (Decision Option A-1). If her analysis of the situation went no further than this, the Secretary could make a decision but would not have addressed the ethical dimensions of the case. Thus, the decision would not be judged an "ethical" one, at least not in the sense of having been made in an ethical manner.

But, the Secretary might come to the same conclusion (that she should resign without protest) by deliberating over the ethical dimensions of the case, and determining that in good conscience she could not implement the policies of the legislature because of the injustices imposed on the clients and employees of the Income Maintenance program (a deontological line of reasoning). At the same time, she might believe that an open protest would continue to bring harm to the agency and to other parts of the Governor's budget, and she should therefore withdraw her own participation but do so without protest. Deliberation, such as just outlined, would be one mark of an ethical decision process and an ethical administrator. As mentioned earlier, to decide to resign without protest out of frustration ("Who needs this?") would not be the result of ethical deliberation and would be a questionable reason for making such a decision.

This illustrates an important point: a decision can be reached through a process of ethical deliberation, or it can be reached through some other process (in this case consideration of political expediency). The chosen course of action might be the same (e.g., to resign without protest) but the justification for the decision would be quite different. The process of arriving at a decision will not adequately justify the decision (i.e., the means will not justify the end) but the process of arriving at a decision *will* influence the reasons for making a decision, and the *reasons* will justify the decision. What has been argued throughout this book is that public administrators must consistently and conscientiously make decisions on the basis of *ethical deliberation* if the ethical tenor of the field is to be improved.

As discussed earlier, the ethical administrator must not adopt a frame of reference for making a decision simply because it

provides a justification for the decision the administrator pre-
fers. Instead, the frame of reference should grow out of a carefully examined and articulated view of the place of moral principles in administrative action. While not everyone will agree
on the frame of reference (e.g., some will use deontological
reasoning while others will use teleological), such agreement is
not necessary for a decision to be accepted as ethical. What is
required is that the administrator make a decision on the basis
of sound reasoning, adequate information and consideration,
and acceptable moral standards. To disagree with a decision
made in this manner is not necessarily to say that it is an
unethical decision.

The Secretary was immediately aware of the moral principles
which could be applied to the decisions of the legislature. She
viewed the policies as unjust and was inclined to resign for
that reason, implying that she would "go public" with those
views (Decision Option A-2). That initial inclination was challenged when she used that same ethical standard (justice) to
judge the implications of resignation. Would it be just to the
other client groups if she were to resign? Would it be just to
compromise her obligations to the Governor and those affected
by other parts of the State budget, by engaging in a public
struggle with the legislature, knowing that they would retaliate
through budget cuts?

To answer these questions, the Secretary must seriously consider the moral principles involved in any course of action she
takes, and try to evaluate the possible consequences. (Even if
one finds a deontological frame of reference most defensible,
consequences of actions are important and need close scrutiny). The case implies that other client groups would suffer
without her leadership, but she must critically evaluate that
conclusion rather than accept it as a given. It is possible that
another equally capable administrator could be appointed to
take her place, and that the legislative initiatives would still be
successful even though she was not in the leadership position.
In addition, the implication that legislative nit-picking of the
Governor's budget is inherently bad for programs must be
evaluated. In fact, such close evaluation of the budget might
be quite justifiable, in which case the Secretary should not view

halting such evaluations as a compelling concern in her deliberations.

In order for the Secretary to make a reasoned and ethical judgment in this case, she might need further information or at least need to give further consideration to other aspects of the case. For example, she must ask herself how much harm would actually come to the income maintenance employees if their caseloads were to be increased. Obviously she believes that they are already being pushed beyond normal limits, but whether a grave injustice is being done to them is another question. Her original position was that she "couldn't live with the budget cuts," but she must now ask herself whether there is a firm moral foundation for that position, or whether it was an expression of frustration more than a moral judgment.

If the deliberation process leads her to conclude that there is no compelling reason to resign her position (or that there are compelling reasons *not* to resign), then the Secretary is left with three options: B-1, to publicly protest; B-2, to accept the decisions of the legislature; and B-3, to discreetly challenge the decisions of the legislature. In choosing Decision Option B-1, the Secretary would probably have to have reached the conclusion that the decisions of the legislature are totally unacceptable from an ethical perspective and that she is morally obligated to challenge those decisions.

If she chooses Decision Option B-2, to accept the decisions of the legislature, this decision would probably be based on the belief that the decisions of the legislature are not morally unacceptable or, at the very least, that potential harm to other client groups or to the Governor's effectiveness outweigh the harm done to employees and clients of the Income Maintenance program.

A question the Secretary of the Department of Social Welfare might ask herself before concluding that she should accept the decision of the legislature is whether her obligation to abide by legitimately formulated public policies (in this case, the legislature's decision about income standards applied to qualifying for income maintenance assistance) is sufficient to justify implementing a policy which she believes is unjust. That question assumes a deontological frame of reference in which a moral principle can adequately justify a decision even though there are undesirable outcomes. Alternatively, from a teleological frame of reference, are the anticipated positive outcomes for other client groups which will result from her continued service as the Secretary sufficient to justify the injustices that will befall the clients and employees of the Income Maintenance program?

As a part of this deliberation, the Secretary must make some judgment about the harm that will come to those potential clients who will be denied welfare because of the new, stricter eligibility policy. Again, the Secretary believes that a legitimate need exists and will not be served under those conditions, but will the families denied welfare payments suffer gravely for having been denied the service? Answering such questions to her own satisfaction might require the Secretary to gather additional data about those potential clients, since a moral judgment cannot always be made in the absence of sufficient empirical information.

It is important to clarify the use of "harm" here. Harm can be thought of as an undesirable consequence, in which case it would be used in a teleological or consequentialist frame of reference. But harm can also have a deontological meaning. For example, "it is morally wrong to inflict avoidable harm on others" is a statement of a moral principle which is accepted by many philosophers. For the Secretary to be concerned about "harm" then, is consistent with either of the two frames of reference.

Another consideration for the Secretary is the precedent that might be set by her decisions, a precedent that can influence not only her own agency in the future but all of State government. For example, does she have reason to believe that her resignation in protest, or remaining in office, but openly protesting the decisions of the legislature, might lead others to act similarly? And would this lead to strained relations between the bureaucracy and the legislature, which would adversely affect state services in the future? If so, does her moral justification for the resignation or the open debate sufficiently justify the potential harm? A question formulated in this way follows closely the reasoning of Kant's "categorical imperative" which, loosely interpreted, asks: If administrators were to universally adopt the decision standard used by the Secretary of the Department of Social Welfare, would it result in a situation that she would be willing to live with?

On the other hand, does she have reason to believe that if she yields to the legislature (Decision Option B-2) when she truly believes they are doing an injustice to those involved with the Income Maintenance program, does her action set a precedent for deferring to authority even when that authority is believed to be wrong? This is a particularly important question as public administration moves toward a higher level of ethical performance. It could be that public administrators would challenge legislative decisions on moral grounds more often, yet few administrators see others doing so and find little support among their peers for such actions. In such a case, the precedent set by a resignation in protest (A-2) or an open challenge of the legislature (B-1) might have far-reaching positive consequences beyond the Department of Social Welfare.

Finally, the Secretary could choose Decision Option B-3, in which she decides to remain in office but to work discreetly to influence the legislature's decisions. This option would be chosen if there is no compelling reason to resign, and no need to set a precedent for other public administrators by openly challenging the legislature. On the other hand, this option also rests on the assumption that the administrator is morally obligated to take some action to influence the legislative decision because that decision is morally wrong. The influence might take the form of providing information to the legislature and influencing them on the basis of professional expertise, or perhaps gaining the support of sympathetic legislators to influence the process. In either case, choosing this option rests on the assumption that the Secretary need not resign, but she cannot ethically allow the issue to pass unchallenged.

An issue not directly addressed to this point is the public administrator's obligation to the "public interest" which includes taxpayers' interests as well as client and employee interests. The situation in question arose because the legislature and the Governor differ in their revenue projections. One question the Secretary might ask herself is whether the legislature's policies regarding income maintenance might be justified if they are correct about the revenue projections and the Governor is wrong. This line of questioning is helpful because if she determines that the policies are unjust regardless of the revenues of the State, then she has an even more compelling ethical justification for protesting them. If her justification is dependent on the Governor's revenue projections being correct, then she has reason to question the moral weight of the case for injustice being done to clients or employees.

## RECOMMENDATIONS

Through the questioning and critical analysis discussed in the previous section, the Secretary will eventually uncover the moral imperatives that underlie the different choices she is faced with. Once those moral imperatives are brought out, she must make a choice among them. The information she has gathered about potential impacts of decisions might provide her with an indication that one course of action will do considerably less harm, or considerably more to promote moral good than the others, in which case she would be likely to choose that course of action. Her information gathering might lead, though, to a situation in which she is faced with competing values and has no evidence to indicate that one choice would be better than another. In this case, she must make a judgment about which value she will give higher priority to.

Ranking moral principles is a particularly difficult endeavor, and one on which there is no high level of consensus. That final decision must be made independently by the administrator but should be tempered by the views and decisions of others in society. For example, if the Secretary determines that she is faced with a value conflict between her commitment to providing a just level of services to the clients in the Income Maintenance program, and her obligation to be loyal to the Governor and the policy process, then she must make a decision about whether justice as a moral principle is more important than loyalty as a moral principle. That decision cannot be made by any other person or group, even a professional ethics committee. And the decision will be subjected to public scrutiny once it has been made, so the Secretary must be confident of her own decision. Clearly defining *why* an administrator should remain loyal to a person, program, agency or procedure opens the act of loyalty to the same ethical critique that other actions and assumptions should be subjected to, and such critique helps to prevent the "organizational imperative" from dictating administrative action.

Answers to all the questions posed in the preceding sections are not available, but certain assumptions will be made as the final decision process is sketched out in what follows.

In arriving at a final decision, the Secretary might first question whether the injustice she originally perceived for those affected by the Income Maintenance program was in fact so serious as to justify a resignation. Unless the increase in caseload for employees and the change in benefits are particularly dramatic, her answer to the question might well be that the consequences will not do grave harm if the legislature's revenue projections are correct. Resigning on that basis, then, would not seem to be justified or at least not necessitated.

That response doesn't address the Secretary's concern, however, that the workers will unionize and the Welfare Mothers' organization will become militant. If the immediate consequences of the legislative action do not cause significant harm, might the ripple effect of unionization and client militancy? There are different responses to this question, depending on one's orientation to unions and to militancy in general, but one response might be that unionization and client militancy are difficult to deal with but not necessarily harmful. In fact, one might argue that the threat of employee unionization and increased client militancy might lead the legislature to do precisely what the Secretary wanted in the first place, but could not achieve on her own. If that is the case, the purposes served by her resignation might be just as effectively accomplished by the actions of others.

This case clearly indicates that the Secretary has cause for concern that injustices are being done through the legislature's policies. But given other problems that are likely to arise should she resign, these injustices are not the only morally compelling issues. Therefore, we might suggest that it is morally justifiable (though not morally necessitated) for her to remain in office and attempt to influence the legislature on these issues through other channels. However, if the situation were of a different sort, perhaps involving the endangerment of lives, or irreparable harm to employees or clients, there *would be* a morally compelling justification for resigning or refusing to implement the policies. That statement reflects a value judgment that respect for life is a higher order moral principle than either obedience to the law or obligations to greater numbers of people when those obligations do not involve the endangerment of life.

If she chooses not to resign, the Secretary still has three possible courses of action. She could openly challenge the legislature, she could discreetly attempt to influence the legislature, or she could choose to accept the legislative decisions. If she decides to remain in the position of Secretary but to challenge the legislature, she would be engaging in open advocacy of policies she believes are best for her constituents. The position is one based on moral principle and conceivably could be justified on those grounds. The consequences of open protest might be, however, that in spite of or because of her actions, the legislature refuses to change its position and in addition makes very deep cuts in other entitlement programs as a form of retaliation. Since the legislature is not the focus of this analysis, the ethics of their actions will not be discussed, but from the Secretary's point of view, she will have taken a morally justified position but have done no significant good for the client group in question, and her actions will have led to potential harm to other client groups. Thus, open protest might be argued to be an ethical position but it is not one that takes into account the impact on the future effectiveness of the Secretary or the agency, which is also morally relevant because it emerges from her obligations to the agency and to the profession. For that reason, it might not be the best action to take.

Again, if the precedent being set by her open objections to the legislature's actions would bring about positive changes in public administration, or if the actions of the legislature are grossly immoral, then there would be more than enough reason for the Secretary to take the stand in question even though it is unlikely that it will be effective in bringing about the desired change. However, in this case the seriousness of the legislative action does not appear to warrant such action.

If the Secretary decides not to resign, and not to openly challenge the actions of the legislature she might justify the choice on the basis that such an action violates no moral imperatives, preserves her ability to serve the needs of all the other client groups in her agency, restores her effectiveness as an administrator, and halts the vengeful budget-cutting the legislature is engaging in as a form of retaliation. In addition, by not publicly challenging the legislature the Secretary is further expressing her loyalty to the Governor by defusing a volatile situation.

One might interpret this decision as being based on a utilitarian (or teleological) justification—the greatest good for the greatest number has been achieved. As argued previously, the criticisms of utilitarianism are sufficiently strong that such a line of reasoning could be inadequate. If, in fact, act utilitarianism has guided the Secretary's decision, this would have allowed the Secretary to make the decision regardless of the degree of harm done to those affected by the Income Maintenance program.

The decision to remain in the position and discreetly protest can also have been arrived at through deontological reasoning: the Secretary is committed to making a just decision and in this case a course of action seeking justice for income maintenance clients might have resulted in a greater injustice to other client groups. A judgment was made about which position would optimize the valued outcome (justice) while not doing irreparable harm to any minority. In addition, such a position permits the public administrator to make a morally justifiable decision and at the same time deal adequately with the practical environment of the bureaucracy, an environment in which there is a great interdependence among the actions of various groups, and where the most preferred decision is not always possible within those constraints.

Given the original inclinations of the administrator and her immediate loyalties to the Income Maintenance program, this would not be an easy decision to reach. And, full acknowledgment must be given to the fact that some harm will come to both the clients and the employees of that program. In addition, the Secretary faces a future of low morale and a potential unionization effort among employees, and further demonstrations by the Welfare Mothers' organization. The Secretary knows they have justifiable concerns, but she also knows that the needs of other client groups will more effectively be met under her leadership than under a changing administration, and that the legislative budgetary process will proceed in a more reasonable manner.

If we assume that the Secretary will not resign her position, and that she will not engage in public debate with the legislature at this time, there is still the possibility of discreet protest. It is imperative that the Secretary take action that will address both the issue of the legislature making policy about employee caseloads, and the issue of eligibility requirements which are too strict (Decision Option B-3). The fact that a choice would be made not to take action in a highly visible way in no way reduces the claims of those affected by the Income Maintenance program. If the Secretary fails to take any action at all, she is failing to meet her professional responsibilities to act on behalf of client groups and employees, and she is implicitly saying that the groups have no moral claim for action. This appears to be contrary to her views of the situation. In fact, the clients and employees of the Income Maintenance program do have some moral justification for their claims, but those claims do not appear to have overriding weight given the other moral issues involved.

## CONCLUSION

Analysis of this case points out the high degree of uncertainty and ambiguity associated with administrative choice, especially regarding moral dilemmas. It is possible to go through a process of deliberation, information gathering, and value ordering which can result in an ethical decision, but the process is a difficult one and there are too few sources of guidance for information and support in making moral choices. This underscores the need for some of the reform measures that were suggested in earlier chapters, particularly those which would have provided intra-organizational support for the administrator who must make these decisions. Had a group of peers been actively involved in discussing and debating ethical issues, she might have been able to discuss the matter with that group and in that way have not only a support system for making a difficult decision, but also the benefit of many points of view. Given that there is no provable "right" answer in decisions about morality, that type of discussion and sharing of viewpoints is particularly helpful to an individual.

A primary source of difficulty in this case rests with the power relationship between the legislature and the public administrator. Such an interpretation of the case supports the contention of earlier chapters, that authority for making decisions should be delegated to the lowest possible level, and that tasks should not be divided in such a way that those who must perform the task have little or no influence on the structure or design of the task. In this case, the legislature's decision regarding caseload violated that caveat and indicates a need for reform. However, there are clearly impediments to reform. Entrenched interests of those involved will lead to significant resistance to such a change in the power and control structure.

Perhaps the legislature could be convinced that such a restructuring of authority is necessary by emphasizing the linkage between this change in the authority structure, and the enhancement of efficiency, effectiveness and organizational productivity. Or, perhaps an enhanced system of accountability would satisfy legislators or any other affected individual or group in authority that the public interest and their own interests could still be served, even with the reform measures in place.

In addition to delegation of authority to the lowest possible levels, it is also helpful to the process of ethical administration if more dialogue were to occur within organizations regarding the values being enhanced by the policies and actions of those in the organization, and the values which underlie the objectives of the organization. Such as ongoing dialogue (perhaps given structure through an "ethics committee" or ongoing administrative development activities dealing with ethics) could provide a forum within which the administrator facing a dilemma such as in the case discussed above, could seek the advice and counsel of peers in making the difficult decision.

Administrators might be better prepared to deal with such dilemmas if more professional and educational efforts were directed toward this. The profession would be called upon to engage in an ongoing dialogue about administrative ethics and also to publish guidelines for the consideration of administrators. *Applying Professional Standards and Ethics in the '80s* (Mertins and Hennigan, 1982) represents a very early step in that direction, but there needs to be continuous effort in that area.

Reform efforts might also include changes within the educational structure of public administration. Professional educators must take it upon themselves to play an active role in preparing their students for the ethical dilemmas they will face as practitioners. Many programs have sought to do this by including the consideration of ethics in such courses as Policy Analysis, and Organization Theory and Behavior. However, this will not sufficiently introduce future professionals to the "way of thinking" that characterizes ethical administration.

The "way of thinking" is not developed simply by raising value questions. There must also be some guidance in seeking answers to those value questions. Achieving success in this effort requires that the teaching of ethical decision making become a fully intentional and integrated part of the educational program. The type of critical ethical analysis that has been suggested here would be greatly enhanced if students were introduced to philosophical concepts which can guide their thinking about situations, and the critique of their own moral convictions as well as critique of public policy. This helps the practitioner to identify ethical issues, to think through those issues using some tools of philosophical analysis, and then to make a decision.

Decisions about ethics must often be made independently and therefore the individual must be prepared to make those decisions. But when discussion and dialogue about the issue is possible, it is important that administrators have a language or vocabulary beyond the organizational language of efficiency and effectiveness in which to carry on the discussion. Public administrators must become as proficient in talking about ethical issues as they are in talking about technical issues. The responsibility for developing that proficiency rests with public administration educators.

An important aspect of that education process is to address the realities of organizational and administrative practice. This is effectively done through the use of case studies such as the one presented and analyzed in this chapter. But, in structuring an educational program it should be acknowledged that it is not just top-level administrators (such as the Secretary in the above case) who face ethical dilemmas. Students and practitioners must also be challenged to recognize the ethical dilemmas in the lowest levels of the authority structure and in the most common of daily activities. For example, the above case includes a passage indicating that the workers at one office had spoken publicly about their support for the Welfare Mothers' organization, and that this action had led to legislative retaliation. What are the ethical issues for those workers? And what are the ethical issues for the case worker who faces as increased caseload but recognizes that he will be unable to provide the same (perhaps not even adequate) levels of service to the clients he serves? By drawing attention to these ethical issues as well as those facing the Secretary, educators will be doing a better job of preparing public administrators to be ethical administrators.

The notion that public administrators must become philosophers as well as managers will meet some resistance, but is nevertheless important if public administration is to become more ethical. This view is supported by several writers who suggest that such a combination of science (whether management, medical, or other science) and philosophy is necessary in order that both will benefit. "Science puts its emphasis on research and verifiable fact. Art and philosophy put the emphasis on creativity and values—values that have something to do with the importance of being human" (Cousins, 1983:144).

In the end, the writer and the physician deal with the uniqueness of human beings and with the need to protect the human condition. Moreover, the physician and the writer need one another: the writer because he can profit from the discipline of testing his facts and slowing down the rush to judgment, and the physician because language is connected to the therapeutic power of attitudes and belief. . . . (Cousins, 1983:144)

Cousins' words are no less applicable to the science of management than to the science of the physician. In order that ethical considerations (value considerations) which are directed at the "whole of the human condition" become a part of administrative practice, the administrator must learn the language of the philosopher, and the philosopher the language of the administrator. Thus, facts can be tested and judgments tempered by moral and ethical considerations. This view was also expressed by Scott and Hart (1979) when they said about professionals challenging the organizational imperative:

Finally, these actions, derived from new attitudes about their life's work, require a foundation in values and a changed perception of the innateness of human nature. This means that in some respects the professionals must become philosophers, and this is a role for which they have not been trained. Yet the philosophical task must precede action. And if philosophers will not become managers, it is certain that managers must become philosophers. (Scott and Hart, 1979:225)

Through the educational process, students can learn the basic language of philosophy, as well as the necessary background in the moral foundations of public administration. Then, as practitioners, they will have a shared language and framework in which to carry on a discussion of ethical issues in public administration. These practitioners should be expected to develop their analytical and ethical judgment skills over a long period of time, as professionals. This requires a strong commitment on the part of practicing administrators to make ethics a central consideration in their actions. Neither organizational nor educational reform can lead to the change necessary without the commitment of practitioners and the profession as a whole.

The "new public administrator" represented a concerned response of the profession at a time when the ethics and values practiced in public administration were being challenged. A renewal of that concern is appropriate now, as we seek to more fully articulate the moral and ethical foundations of public administration, in order that this may serve as a guide for administrative action in the decades to come.

# BIBLIOGRAPHY

Abelson, Raziel, and Nielsen, Kai. "History of Ethics." *The Encyclopedia of Philosophy*, Vol. 3. New York: The Macmillan Co. and The Free Press, 1967, pp. 81–117.

Adler, Mortimer J. *Six Great Ideas*. New York: Macmillan Publishing Co., 1981.

Albert, Ethel M., Demise, Theodore C., and Peterfreund, Sheldon P. *Great Traditions in Ethics*. New York: D. Van Nostrand Co., 1969.

Anderson, Hurst R. "Ethical Values in Administration." *Personnel Administration* 17 (January 1954): 1–12.

Arendt, Hannah. *Between Past and Future*. New York: The Viking Press, 1961.

Baier, Kurt. *The Moral Point of View: A Rational Basis of Ethics*, abr. ed. New York: Random House, 1965.

Barnet, Richard J., and Muller, Ronald E. *Global Reach: The Power of the Multinational Corporations*. New York: Simon and Schuster, 1974.

Bendor, Jonathan, Taylor, Serce, and Van Gaalen, Roland. "Bureaucratic Expertise versus Legislative Authority: A Model of Deception and Monitoring in Budgeting." *American Political Science Review* 79 (December 1985): 1041–1060.

Bernstein, Richard J. *The Restructuring of Social and Political Theory.* New York: Harcourt Brace Jovanovich, 1976.

Bok, Sissela. *Lying: Moral Choice in Public and Private Life.* New York: Vintage Books, 1978.

Boling, T. Edwin, and Dempsey, Jack. "Ethical Dilemmas in Government: Designing an Organizational Response." *Public Personnel Management* 10, no. 1 (1981): 11–19.

Bowman, James S. "Ethical Issues for the Public Manager." In *Handbook of Organization Management*, ed. William B. Eddy. New York: Marcel Dekker, 1983a, pp. 69–102.

————. "Whistle Blowing: Literature and Resource Materials." *Public Administration Review* 43 (May/June 1983b): 271–276.

————. "Managerial Ethics in Business and Government." *Business Horizons* 19 (October 1976): 48–54.

Brandt, Richard B. "Some Merits of One Form of Rule Utilitarianism." In *Mill: Utilitarianism with Critical Essays*, ed. Samuel Gorovitz. Indianapolis: Bobbs-Merrill, 1971, pp. 324–344.

————. *Ethical Theory: The Problems of Normative and Critical Ethics.* Englewood Cliffs, N.J.: Prentice-Hall, 1959.

Chandler, Ralph Clark. "The Civil Servant as Trustee: A Reorganization of the Professionalism Discussion." *Dialogue* 5 (Summer 1983a): 5–21.

————. "The Problem of Moral Reasoning in American Public Administration: The Case for a Code of Ethics." *Public Administration Review* 43 (January/February 1983b): 32–39.

Commager, Henry Steele, ed. *Selections from The Federalist.* New York: Appleton-Century-Crofts, 1949.

Cooper, Terry L. *The Responsible Administrator.* Port Washington, N.Y.: Kennikat Press, 1982; rev. ed. New York: Associated Faculty Press, 1986.

Cousins, Norman. *The Healing Heart.* New York: W. W. Norton and Co., 1983.

Davis, Kenneth Culp. *Discretionary Justice: A Preliminary Inquiry.* Baton Rouge: Louisiana State University Press, 1969.

De Beauvoir, Simone. *The Ethics of Ambiguity*, trans. Bernard Frechtman. Secaucus, N.J.: The Citadel Press, 1948.

DeGeorge, Richard T. "Moral Issues in Business." In *Ethics, Free Enterprise and Public Policy*, ed. Richard T. DeGeorge and Joseph A. Pichler. New York: Oxford University Press, 1978, pp. 3–18.

Denhardt, Robert B. *In the Shadow of Organization*. Lawrence, Kans.: The Regents Press of Kansas, 1981.

————. "Organizational Citizenship and Personal Freedom." *Public Administration Review* 28 (January/February 1968): 47–54.

Dennony, Michael. "The Privilege of Ourselves: Hannah Arendt on Judgment." In *Hannah Arendt: The Recovery of the Public World*, ed. Melvin A. Hill. New York: St. Martin's Press, 1979.

Donaldson, Thomas, and Werhane, Patricia H. *Ethical Issues in Business, A Philosophical Approach*. 2d ed. Englewood Cliffs, N.J.: Prentice-Hall, 1983.

Feldman, Fred. *Introductory Ethics*. Englewood Cliffs, N.J.: Prentice-Hall, 1978.

Fischer, Frank. "Ethical Discourse in Public Administration." *Administration and Society* 15 (May 1983): 5–42.

Fleishman, Joel L., and Payne, Bruce L. *Ethical Dilemmas and the Education of Policymakers*. Hastings-on-Hudson, N.Y.: The Hastings Center, 1980.

Frankena, William K. *Ethics*. 2d ed. Englewood Cliffs, N.J.: Prentice-Hall, 1973.

Frederickson, H. George, and Chandler, Ralph Clark, eds. "Citizenship and Public Administration." *Public Administration Review* (March 1984).

Garnett, A. Campbell. *Ethics: A Critical Introduction*. New York: The Ronald Press Co., 1960.

Gawthrop, Louis C. *Public Sector Management, Systems, and Ethics*. Bloomington: Indiana University Press, 1984.

Goldman, Alan H. *The Moral Foundation of Professional Ethics*. Totowa, N.J.: Rowman and Littlefield, 1980.

Golembiewski, Robert T. *Men, Management, and Morality: Toward a New Organizational Ethic*. New York: McGraw-Hill Book Co., 1965.

Goodin, Robert E. "Vulnerabilities and Responsibilities: An Ethical Defense of the Welfare State." *American Political Science Review* 79 (September 1985): 775–787.

Goodpaster, Kenneth, and Matthews, John B., Jr. "Can a Corporation Have a Conscience?" *Harvard Business Review* 60 (January/February 1982): 132–141.

Gouinlock, James. *The Moral Writings of John Dewey*. New York: Hafner Press, 1976.

Hampshire, Stuart et al. *Public & Private Morality*. Cambridge: Cambridge University Press, 1978.

Harmon, Michael M. "Normative Theory and Public Administration:

Some Suggestions for a Redefinition of Administrative Responsibility." In *Toward a New Public Administration*, ed. Frank Marini. Scranton, Pa.: Chandler Publishing Co., 1971, pp. 172–185.

Hart, David K. "Social Equity, Justice and the Equitable Administrator." *Public Administration Review* 34 (January/February 1974): 3–10.

Hays, Steven W., and Gleissner, Richard R. "Codes of Ethics in State Government: A Nationwide Survey." *Public Personnel Management* 10, no. 1 (1981): 48–58.

Hegel, Georg Wilhelm Friedrick. *The Philosophy of History*. New York: Dover Publications, 1956.

Henry, Nicholas. *Public Administration and Public Affairs*. Englewood Cliffs, N.J.: Prentice-Hall, 1975.

Howton, F. William. *Functionaries*. Chicago: Quadrangle Books, 1969.

Hummel, Ralph P. *The Bureaucratic Experience*. New York: St. Martin's Press, 1977.

Jaques, Elliott. *A General Theory of Bureaucracy*. New York: Halstead Press, 1976.

Kant, Immanuel. *Critique of Judgment*. New York: Hafner Publishing Co., 1951.

Kaufman, Herbert. *The Administrative Behavior of Federal Bureau Chiefs*. Washington, D.C.: The Brookings Institution, 1981.

Kingdon, John W. *Agendas, Alternatives, and Public Policies*. Boston: Little, Brown and Co., 1984.

Kohlberg, Lawrence. "Stage and Sequence: The Cognitive-Developmental Approach to Socialization." In *Handbook of Socialization Theory and Research*, ed. David A. Goslin. Chicago: Rand McNally and Co., 1969, pp. 347–480.

Kuhn, Thomas S. *The Structure of Scientific Revolutions*. 2d ed. Chicago: University of Chicago Press, 1970.

Ladd, John. "Morality and the Ideal of Rationality in Formal Organizations." In *Ethical Issues in Business, A Philosophical Approach*, ed. Thomas Donaldson and Patricia H. Werhane. 2d. ed. Englewood Cliffs, N.J.: Prentice-Hall, 1983, pp. 125–136.

Leys, Wayne A. R. *Ethics for Policy Decisions*. New York: Prentice-Hall, 1952.

————. *Ethics and Social Policy*. New York: Prentice-Hall, 1944.

Lilla, Mark T. "Ethos, 'Ethics,' and Public Service." *The Public Interest* (Spring 1981): 3–17.

Lipsky, Michael. *Street Level Bureaucracy: Dilemmas of the Individual in Public Service*. New York: Russell Sage Foundation, 1980.

Locke, John. *The Second Treatise of Government*. Indianapolis: Bobbs-Merrill, 1952.

Lowi, Theodore. *The End of Liberalism*. New York: Norton, 1969.

MacIntyre, Alasdair, *After Virtue: A Study of Moral Theory*, 2d. ed. Notre Dame, Ind.: University of Notre Dame Press, 1984.

Marini, Frank, ed. *Toward a New Public Administration: The Minnowbrook Perspective*. Scranton, Pa.: Chandler Publishing Co., 1971.

Marx, Fritz Morstein. "Administrative Ethics and the Rule of Law." *The American Political Science Review* 43 (December 1949): 1119–1144.

Means, Richard L. *The Ethical Imperative: The Crisis in American Values*. Garden City, N.Y.: Doubleday and Co., 1969.

Meier, Kenneth J. *Politics and the Bureaucracy: Policymaking in the Fourth Branch of Government*. Scituate, Mass.: Duxbury Press, 1979.

Menzies, Isabel E. P. "A Case Study in the Functioning of Social Systems as a Defense against Anxiety." *Human Relations* 13 (1960): 95–121.

Mertins, Herman, Jr., and Hennigan, Patrick J., eds. *Applying Professional Standards and Ethics in the '80s: A Workbook and Study Guide for Public Administrators*. Washington, D.C.: American Society for Public Administration, 1982.

Mill, John Stuart. *Utilitarianism*, ed. Oskar Piest. New York: Bobbs-Merrill, 1957.

Nakamura, Robert T., and Smallwood, Frank. *The Politics of Policy Implementation*. New York: St. Martin's Press, 1980.

Nigro, Felix A., and Nigro, Lloyd G. *The New Public Personnel Administration*. Itascu, Ill.: F. E. Peacock Publishers, 1976.

Pastin, Mark. *The Hard Problems of Management: Gaining the Ethics Edge*. San Francisco: Jossey-Bass, 1986.

Rabin, Jack, and Bowman, James S., eds. *Politics and Administration*. New York: Marcel Dekker, 1984.

Rawls, John. *A Theory of Justice*. Cambridge, Mass.: The Belknap Press of Harvard University Press, 1971.

Redford, Emmette S. *Democracy in the Administrative State*. New York: Oxford University Press, 1969.

Rizzo, Ann-Marie, and Patka, Thomas J. "The Organizational Imperative and Supervisory Control: Their Effects on Managerial Ethics." *Public Personnel Management* 10, no. 1 (1981): 103–109.

Rohr, John A. "Ethics in Public Administration: A 'State of the Discipline' Report." Presented to the 1986 Annual Meeting of the American Society for Public Administration, Anaheim, Calif., April 1986a.

————. *To Run a Constitution: The Legitimacy of the Administrative State.* Lawrence, Kans: University of Kansas Press, 1986b.

————. *Ethics for Bureaucrats: An Essay on Law and Values.* New York: Marcel Dekker, 1978.

Rose-Ackerman, Susan. *Corruption: A Study in Political Economy.* New York: Academic Press, 1978.

Rosen, Bernard. *Holding Government Bureaucracies Accountable.* New York: Praeger Publishers, 1982.

Schmidt, Warren H., and Posner, Barry Z. "Values and Expectations of Federal Service Executives." *Public Administration Review* 46 (September/October 1986): 447–454.

Scott, William G., and Hart, David K. *Organizational America.* Boston: Houghton Mifflin Co., 1979.

Sibley, Mulford Q. *Political Ideas and Ideologies: A History of Political Thought.* New York: Harper & Row, 1970.

Simon, Herbert. *Administrative Behavior.* New York: Macmillan, 1948.

Singer, Peter. *Democracy and Disobedience.* New York: Oxford University Press, 1974.

Smith, Adam. *The Theory of Moral Sentiments*, ed. D. D. Raphael and A. L. Macfie. Indianapolis: Liberty Classics, 1982.

Stewart, Debra W. "Ethics and the Profession of Public Administration: The Moral Responsibility of Individuals in Public Sector Organizations." *Public Administration Quarterly* 45 (Winter 1985a): 487–495.

————. "Professionalism vs Democracy: Friedrich vs Finer Revisited." *Public Administration Quarterly* 45 (Spring 1985b): 13–25.

"Terminal Proceduritis," *Wall Street Journal* (September 21, 1983), p. 32.

Thayer, Fred C. "Comments on Chandler's 'The Problem of Moral Illiteracy in Professional Discourse.' " *Dialogue* 5 (Fall 1982): 17–18.

Thompson, Dennis F. "The Possibility of Administrative Ethics." *Public Administration Review* 45 (September/October 1985): 555–561.

Thompson, James D. *Organization in Action.* New York: McGraw-Hill Book Co., 1967.

Truelson, Judith. "Protecting David from Goliath: On Blowing the Whistle on Systemic Corruption." *Dialogue* 8 (Spring 1986): 1–23.

Useem, Michael. *The Inner Circle.* New York: Oxford University Press, 1984.

Vickers, Sir Geoffrey. *The Art of Judgment.* New York: Basic Books, 1965.

Wakefield, Susan. "Ethics and the Public Service: A Case for Individual Responsibility." *Public Administration Review* 36 (November/December 1976): 661–666.

Waldo, Dwight. *The Enterprise of Public Administration*. Novato, Calif.: Chandler and Sharp Publishers, 1980.

Weber, Max. *The Theory of Social and Economic Organization*. New York: The Free Press, 1947.

Wilson, Woodrow. "The Study of Administration." Reprinted in *Classics of Public Administration*, ed. Jay M. Shafritz and Albert C. Hyde. Oak Park, Ill.: Moor Publishing Co., 1978, pp. 3–17.

Yarwood, Dean L. "The Ethical World of Organizational Professionals and Scientists." *Public Administration Quarterly* 45 (Winter 1985): 461–486.

Yates, Douglas T. Jr. "Hard Choices: Justifying Bureaucratic Decisions." In *Public Duties: The Moral Obligations of Government Officials*, ed. Joel L. Fleishman, Lance Liebman, and Mark H. Moore. Cambridge, Mass.: Harvard University Press, 1981, pp. 32–51.

# INDEX

**About the Author**

KATHRYN G. DENHARDT is Visiting Assistant Professor of Public Administration at the University of Missouri at Columbia. Her articles have appeared in *Administration and Society*.